Oxford School Shakespeare

Much Ado About Nothing

Edited by

Roma Gill, OBE
M.A. *Cantab.*, B. Litt. *Oxon*

OXFORD
UNIVERSITY PRESS

OXFORD
UNIVERSITY PRESS

Great Clarendon Street, Oxford OX2 6DP

Oxford University Press is a department of the University of Oxford.
It furthers the University's objective of excellence in research, scholarship,
and education by publishing worldwide in

Oxford New York

Athens Auckland Bangkok Bogotá Buenos Aires Calcutta
Cape Town Chennai Dar es Salaam Delhi Florence Hong Kong Istanbul
Karachi Kuala Lumpur Madrid Melbourne Mexico City Mumbai
Nairobi Paris São Paulo Singapore Taipei Tokyo Toronto Warsaw
with associated companies in Berlin Ibadan

Oxford is a registered trade mark of Oxford University Press
in the UK and in certain other countries

© Oxford University Press 1999

ISBN 0 19 832007 8 (Schools edition)
ISBN 0 19 832008 6 (Trade edition)

Illustrations by Alexy Pendle

Cover photograph by Donald Cooper shows Sinead Cusack as Beatrice and
Derek Jacobi as Benedick in the Royal Shakespeare Company's 1984 production of
Much Ado About Nothing.

For Katy

Oxford School Shakespeare
edited by Roma Gill

Typeset by Herb Bowes Graphics, Oxford
Printed in Great Britain at the University Press, Cambridge

Contents

Women in Love

Are you in love? Have you ever been in love—or do you hope one day to fall in love? Answer 'Yes' (privately) to any one of these questions, and you can read *Much Ado About Nothing* with sympathy. Answer 'No'—and you can laugh to see how easily others can be beguiled. (But beware! You may not escape all that easily.)

Shakespeare's imagination knew love in all its moods—from its first surprised awakening to its final hopeless despair, from the comedy of love discovered to the tragedy of love lost for ever. No one knew better than he that 'The course of true love never did run smooth'[1], and love is a major theme—often the only theme—in more than twenty of his plays, in both his narrative poems, and in almost all of the 154 sonnets.

In eight early plays, all of them comedies, Shakespeare develops and contrasts the love affairs of two young women—one small and dark, the other tall and fair—with their respective partners (who are usually far less interesting than the women themselves). For each play the action is basically the same: a love is declared, is challenged, and is finally reasserted into the harmony of marriage. Although the titles of the plays may suggest that their subjects are unimportant (*As You Like It*, *Twelfth Night—or What You Will*), the poetry communicates intense emotions and shows the dramatist to be fully engaged with his characters, and deeply concerned about them.

Much Ado About Nothing is the last of these plays, and its title, apparently making a pun on 'nothing' and 'noting' (which had the same pronunciation in Shakespeare's day), seems to question its own seriousness. 'Nothing'? 'Men were deceivers ever'? Slander and misrepresentation are among Shakespeare's greatest evils, for which there can be no forgiveness and which, in *Othello*, will give rise to one of his greatest tragedies. *Much Ado* foreshadows this, anticipating the darker humour which will dominate the next phase of Shakespeare's writing until he reaches the serenity of the final romances.

---

[1] *A Midsummer Night's Dream*, *1*, 1, 134.

For the present, however, the end of the play is laughter and dancing. Hero's near-tragedy is subordinated to the polished prose and high delight of Beatrice and Benedick who, ever since the seventeenth century, have taken precedence in audience esteem—

> . . . let but Beatrice
> And Benedick be seen, lo in a trice
> The Cockpit, galleries, boxes, are all full . . .

Leonard Digges
(1640; prefatory poem for Shakespeare's *Poems*)

Leading Characters of the Play

Don Pedro The Prince of Aragon. He has won a victory over his illegitimate brother, and is visiting Messina on his way home.

Don John The illegitimate brother of Don Pedro. A stage direction describes him as 'the Bastard', and he describes himself as 'a plain-dealing villain'.

Claudio A young nobleman who has acquitted himself well in the recent fighting, but is still very immature and naive in his judgements and conduct.

Benedick A follower of the prince, whose name (*benedictus*) means 'the blessed one'. He has adopted a pose of woman-hater, and swears he will never marry.

Borachio A follower and friend of Don John, and the originator of the scheme to discredit Hero. His name comes from the Spanish word for 'wine-bottle'.

Leonato The governor of Messina and father of Hero. He is flattered by the attentions of Don Pedro, and quick to believe whatever the prince tells him.

Hero The daughter of Leonato, described by Claudio as 'a modest young lady', and dismissed by Benedick as 'too low for a high praise, and too little for a great praise'. Her name may have been suggested by *Hero and Leander*, a narrative poem (published 1598) by Christopher Marlowe, which tells of the meetings of two lovers (in Greek mythology) who were separated by the Hellespont.

Beatrice Although Leonato is 'her uncle and her guardian', the position of Beatrice in the family and household is unclear. She speaks and behaves with more than usual freedom, and her witty intelligence presents a challenge to all the male characters. Her name, like that of Benedick, means 'the blessed one' (*beatrix*), and she too has sworn never to marry.

Dogberry Master Constable of Messina. He has a great opinion of himself and his office but has an imperfect mastery of the English language. The role was designed for Will Kemp, a famous and accomplished actor of low-comedy roles.

Verges Headborough (=under-constable). Dogberry's assistant, and Kemp's 'straight man'. The role was designed for Richard Cowley, another comic actor whose pale complexion and scrawny limbs, contrasting with the burly physique of Will Kemp, may have suggested the character's name—'verjuice' was the vinegary, acid juice of unripe fruit, used medicinally and in cooking.

Synopsis

Much Ado About Nothing: commentary

Act 1

Scene 1 The happy opening of the scene establishes an atmosphere which will continue—though not unbroken—throughout the play. An easy, relaxed prose creates a civilized society, courtly in manners, but free from the court's formality (as suggested in the affected speech of the messenger), and always ready to burst from wit to laughter.

Leonato, the governor of Messina, is delighted to welcome and entertain the Prince of Aragon, whilst Hero and Beatrice, Leonato's daughter and niece, look forward to receiving the prince's followers. In appearance and temperament the two girls are very different: dark-haired Hero, small and quiet, contrasts with the vivacious Beatrice, tall, fair—and probably somewhat older. Beatrice is eager for news, interrupting the elaborate courtesies of the messenger and deliberately mistaking his careful speeches until the poor man, bewildered by such unladylike behaviour, is rescued by Hero and Leonato, who are listening in amusement. Their conversation allows time for the prince's party to catch up with their herald and appear on the stage.

Already the audience knows enough to identify the different characters: Don Pedro of Aragon, victorious from a recent battle; a young officer called Claudio who has acquitted himself with distinction in the fighting; and the object of Beatrice's interest, 'Signor Montanto'—otherwise known as 'Signor Benedick of Padua'—who engages immediately with her in a quickfire exchange of insults. Both are determinedly single, professing themselves haters of marriage and making it clear that they have no attachments: 'truly I love none' says Benedick, and Beatrice is quick to agree—'I thank God and my cold blood I am of your humour'.

Also in the prince's entourage is a man who, amidst the general warmth of greeting, stands cold and aloof. A shadow seems to pass over the company to hear his abrupt acknowledgement of Leonato's hospitality, but this is dispersed when Leonato and Don

Pedro, yielding and offering precedence, go hand-in-hand into the house.

Claudio, however, detains Benedick with man-to-man confidences concerning Leonato's daughter, a 'modest young lady' for whom he has conceived a most poetic passion which is not to be quenched by the cold water of Benedick's scorn. Marriage, to Benedick, means cuckoldry—a pitiful state for those involved, but a constant source of amusement for outsiders—and he is comically horrified and disappointed to find that it has robbed him of yet another 'sworn brother'. The scepticism of Don Pedro, returning to seek his companions, provokes Benedick's misogyny to further extravagances—and the audience waits happily for the catastrophic turn of events that will show us 'Benedick, the married man'.

Tactfully despatching Benedick on some (probably unnecessary) errand, Don Pedro can turn his attentions to Claudio, who speaks the first verse line of the play as the mood changes from everyday banter and friendly courtesy to serious discussion for a matter of great importance.

My liege, your highness now may do me good. (line 264)

Claudio's love seems to be diplomatic as well as passionate: his social status and his military career have both been taken into consideration before the 'soft and delicate desires' were allowed to prompt his present approach to Don Pedro. Perhaps the conventions of his society require that such affairs are conducted through an intermediary—or perhaps Claudio is too shy to address Hero for himself! But assistance is freely offered: Don Pedro will be his spokesman and, disguised as Claudio in the 'revelling' promised for that same evening, he will declare his love and win Hero's heart.

The stage is set, the characters are prepared—and the audience can have little doubt about the final outcome. But the best laid plans often go astray, mistakes are easily made . . .

Scene 2　. . . and Don Pedro's words, overheard even though they were spoken in the seclusion of a 'thick-pleached alley', have been misunderstood. Leonato is busy, but he will make sure that Hero is prepared to receive a *royal* proposal. This mistake was innocent enough—but there is worse to follow because . . .

Scene 3　. . . another listener, with more accurate hearing, was hiding 'behind the arras' of a 'musty room' (perhaps there was more than one conversation). Now Borachio reports his intelligence to Don

John, lifting him out of his depression so that he can identify his own character and his function in the play: 'I am a plain-dealing villain'. Evil, full-blooded melodramatic evil, has come into the happy world of Leonato's Messina and is directed, with Don John's bitter, sardonic humour, at 'the most exquisite Claudio', the 'young start-up' who has 'all the glory of [his] overthrow'. Gleefully meditating revenge, Don John the Bastard leads his informer into Leonato's 'great supper'.

Act 2

Scene 1   After their supper, the family reassembles. Beatrice (perhaps a little drunk?) is happily abandoned to her own wit as she flirts with the old men in a conversation where the horns of cuckoldry are once again a main source of amusement. In this society, it seems, women as well as men assume that faithlessness is inevitable among married couples. Hero, however, is silent: she cannot share in the freedom that Beatrice enjoys through having no parents to frame her destiny, and knows that she must be 'ruled by [her] father'— who, believing what Antonio told him, has prepared his daughter to receive a proposal from the prince himself.

The guests come together, and the evening's 'revelling'—a masked ball—begins. Such entertainments were popular with the Elizabethans, perhaps because the masks (which could be elaborate, or grotesque) gave more than usual licence to those who joined in the fun—as we see here. As each couple comes downstage, the audience, for a moment, overhears the different conversations. Don Pedro's meaning we can understand—but Hero's responses are ambivalent; Balthasar makes an approach to Margaret (who rejects him) and Ursula is cheeky to old Antonio; Beatrice, perhaps recognizing Benedick, takes the opportunity to taunt and even insult him—and his mask cannot cover the dismay and hurt that he feels.

Outside the dance and wearing no festive mask, Don John pretends to mistake the disguised Claudio for Benedick and tells him that Don Pedro is courting Hero—for himself! Borachio is quick to give support to the falsehood, and Claudio is even more convinced of his betrayal when Benedick (himself deceived by appearances) offers his condolences. Like a boy thinking himself beaten by a man, Claudio surrenders his claims with no further argument: he lacks strength and resources to fight back. Luckily he has a friend—and respect for Benedick increases as (despite his own hurt) he takes up Claudio's cause, tactfully reproaching his prince for unsporting behaviour. Don Pedro soon puts his mind at rest—and then listens to Benedick's own complaint as he explodes in semi-comic wrath.

Benedick has been stung to the quick, utterly demoralized, his manhood threatened—and he hides his embarrassment in a rapid escape when Beatrice approaches, leaving Don Pedro to remonstrate with her on his behalf. But the reproaches meet with careless dismissal from an unrepentant Beatrice, who hints at an earlier injustice that she had received from Benedick when he 'won [her heart] with false dice' (and which has perhaps occasioned her present tartness).

Beatrice has brought with her the bruised Claudio, now sullen and submissive before the prince. Even after the mistake has been cleared up, he seems unable to speak for himself, and needs to be urged on by Beatrice to take Hero by the hand for a little, deceptively simple, ceremony. Here the formal language is enough, with the token kiss that is given and received, to constitute a legally binding 'marriage by pre-contract':

Leonato
Count, take of me my daughter, and with her my fortunes. His grace hath made the match, and all grace say amen to it.

Claudio
Lady, as you are mine, I am yours.

The solemnity is intense, but momentary—and soon dissolved by Beatrice, who looks on the happy couple and compares her own single condition with words that may not be altogether light-hearted. She easily turns away Don Pedro's (half-serious) offer, however: 'Your grace is too costly to wear every day', and obeys her uncle's dismissal to household duties—'will you look to those things I told you of?'

When Beatrice has left the room Don Pedro voices the thought that must be in every audience's heart: 'She were an excellent wife for Benedick.' Once more Don Pedro will be a go-between—but this time for two reluctant lovers.

Scene 2   From one plot to another—but how different in tone and intention! Don John's hatred has grown until he is 'sick in displeasure', and he will snatch at any suggestion to hurt Claudio—who will be made to think that he is mocked, as well as betrayed, when he hears the supposed Hero call an unknown midnight suitor by his name.

Don John's malice may seem somewhat slow to appreciate Borachio's scheme, but it is important that the audience should know all the details: we shall never *see* the much-discussed rendezvous, and there is no time to ask awkward questions (just how is Borachio going to 'fashion the matter' so that Hero is not in her chamber on the night before her wedding?) because we are quickly presented with . . .

Scene 3   . . . another virtuoso performance from Benedick as he laments the change in Claudio and his own loss of a soldier-friend—yet another 'sworn brother' lost to matrimony whilst he enjoys his bachelor freedom! But the freedom and his pleasure in it will be short-lived, for the prince and Claudio, with music and poetry, begin to lay their siege—using love's proper medium, verse, before changing back to prose for their plotting. At first their attempts are clumsy but, with a little nudging and urging, they manage to persuade Leonato, from his privileged position as Hero's confidant, to provide them with evidence of Beatrice's love: 'My daughter tells us all.' Praise for Beatrice and criticism of himself convince Benedick the misogynist to recant his position—'When I said I would die a bachelor, I did not think I should live till I were married'—and when Beatrice comes reluctantly to call him to dinner, he slips somewhat awkwardly into the lover's role and thanks her with a regular verse line: 'Fair Beatrice, I thank you for your pains.'

Interpreting Beatrice's answers to suit his altered opinion of her, and encouraged by his own arguments, Benedick takes a positive step forward: 'I will go get her picture.'

Act 3

Scene 1   The second stage of Don Pedro's scheme runs smoothly from the very beginning. Hero, having despatched Margaret to fetch Beatrice, takes evident delight in talking over her cousin's faults and failings with Ursula (who is perhaps slightly higher in social esteem than Margaret). The gentle Hero, hitherto placid and docile, proves a sharp critic and her words, however intended, are hurtful: Beatrice is 'so self-endear'd . . . so odd and from all fashions' that her conduct 'cannot be commendable', and Benedick, loving her not wisely but too well, should be counselled 'to fight against his passion' and rather 'waste inwardly' than 'die with mocks'. Ursula, tongue in cheek, attempts to mitigate Hero's censure: Beatrice 'cannot be so much without true judgement' as to reject Signor Benedick, who is 'foremost in report through Italy'.

Beatrice, listening behind the same stage property (now a 'pleachèd bower') that had concealed Benedick, is immediately stricken with remorse and love—a love which expresses itself in an almost-sonnet (two quatrains and a couplet) whose verse deftly closes up the scene.

Scene 2 Smartened up and newly shaven (Beatrice 'could not endure a husband with a beard on his face'—*2, 1, 28*), Benedick takes Leonato away for 'eight or nine wise words'—much to the amusement of Don Pedro and Claudio. But the gloomy Don John, his malice disguised as duty and favour, breaks into their delight with strange insinuations, bemoaning the 'suit ill spent, and labour ill bestowed' that has linked Claudio with Hero—'Leonato's Hero, your Hero, every man's Hero'. Each repetition of her name adds force to the accusations, and he describes the (wholly imaginary) scene at the bedchamber window in such detail that his words alone are enough to convince his hearers of Hero's guilt. The scene ends in an operatic chorus of lamentation—

Don Pedro
O day untowardly turned!

Claudio
O mischief strangely thwarting!

Don John
O plague right well prevented!

But before the audience can worry unduly about the sudden alteration in Claudio, the mood of the play switches from high melodrama to low comedy.

Scene 3 A comic interlude allows for time to pass . . . Dogberry, Master Constable, assembles the Watch for a briefing on the night's duties, his self-importance bursting through his speech in grand malapropisms—mistaken words that sometimes express the opposite of the intended meaning ('desertless' for 'deserving', 'tolerable' for 'intolerable'). The police force is made up of unpaid local citizens chosen for these duties (which might be avoided by paying for a substitute), and their incompetence was proverbial—an easy source of entertainment for any humorist, but particularly useful now for Shakespeare's purposes!

Don John's scheme has been put into operation, and now Borachio, drunk with success, boasts of his performance in the charade that has deceived Claudio and Don Pedro. Conrad, bemused by talk of 'fashion' as a 'deformed thief' that can alter a man's appearance, is slow to understand, forcing Borachio to explain exactly what has happened—and what is going to happen the next morning when Claudio meets Hero, 'as he was appointed'.

The Watch have heard enough, and in the arrest of Borachio and Conrad the audience knows that they have indeed 'recovered the most dangerous piece of lechery that ever was known in the commonwealth'. But it is with heightened suspense that we watch Hero preparing for her wedding.

Scene 4   She is understandably nervous and irritable, oddly depressed—'my heart is exceeding heavy'—and impatient with Margaret's bawdy jokes, which are further fuelled when Beatrice starts snuffling about her cold. Margaret immediately guesses the cause, and her fun with *carduus benedictus* (the 'holy thistle' cure-all remedy) begins to arouse Beatrice's suspicions. But time is running short . . .

Scene 5   . . . and elsewhere in the house Leonato is far too busy to listen to Dogberry's ramblings, and the 'examination' of the 'two auspicious persons' has to be delegated to the delighted Dogberry.

Act 4

Scene 1   Disaster, we know, must come soon, and the audience welcomes Leonato's injunction to Friar Francis to 'be brief', but even our foreknowledge does not entirely mitigate the shock of Claudio's curt answer to the friar's question:

> **Friar**
> You come hither, my lord, to marry this lady?
> **Claudio**
>   No.

The ceremonious opening (which would be reinforced by appropriate stage properties) quickly degenerates in the heat of Claudio's anger. His accusations slap across Hero's face, and the word 'maid' spits out with vicious repetition in the stinging verse lines. Claudio has (he feels) been deeply insulted, and the nervous under-current of sexual unease that once rippled and bubbled through the play in jokes about cuckolds' horns is now in full flood, bearing down all before it, at the thought of being married to 'an approved wanton'. Don Pedro, believing himself equally 'dishonoured' for having tried to 'link [his] dear friend to a common stale', adds his authority and evidence, and Don John's hypocrisy lends a final smear of slime—

> Thus, pretty lady,
> I am sorry for thy much misgovernment

—before he hurries Claudio and his brother away from the scene, leaving Hero collapsed upon the ground.

   Benedick, however, does not go out with his friend and his prince—an obvious sign of his changed allegiance—and tries to keep calm whilst Leonato, instantly convinced by Don Pedro of his daughter's guilt, abandons himself to bitter self-pity. Beatrice has no doubts about Hero's innocence, and her certainty is shared by Friar Francis, who sets the weight of his training and experience against the superficial judgements that have condemned her:

> Trust not my age,
> My reverence, calling, nor divinity,
> If this sweet lady lie not guiltless here.

Leonato is half-satisfied, and—after it has been explained to him at some length—falls in with the friar's scheme for a second deception of Claudio.

The long explanation serves also to transpose the shocked feelings of an audience into a different key, ready to enjoy the moment we have all been waiting for. In her first distress Beatrice had looked for help from 'Signor Benedick', and now Benedick comes to her aid. The blank verse of tragedy changes, through the rhymed quatrain with which Friar Francis patches up the exit of Hero and Leonato, to prose for the wordplay which is the habitual—perhaps the only—means by which Beatrice and Benedick can communicate with each other.

Very gently, they lead each other into their declarations of love and then, in love's security, Beatrice makes the testing demand on Benedick: 'Kill Claudio'. The actress can make what she will of this line, but Benedick must know that his response will be crucial for his relationships both with Beatrice and with his former associates. The decision is soon made, and action will be taken . . .

Scene 2 . . . but meanwhile Dogberry is blundering his way through the interrogation of Conrad and Borachio until the sexton, exasperated, intervenes. He already knows what happened in the church earlier that morning, and can confront the 'false knaves' with the truth—and with the additional information that Don John 'is secretly stolen away'. Conrad (who does not, after all, share Borachio's guilt) shakes off Dogberry's arrest with impatience—and provides Dogberry with the cue for a verbal explosion that will re-echo until his very last appearance: 'O that I had been writ down an ass!'

Act 5

Scene 1 Leonato's grief knows no limits, refusing to allow Antonio to speak any comfort until some kind of revenge is hinted—then suddenly his note is changed: 'My soul doth tell me Hero is belied, And that shall Claudio know . . . ' Claudio (who seems not to have heard of Hero's 'death') is hurrying off somewhere with Don Pedro, but Leonato, using the 'thou' form of contempt, lays home his charge. A brawl is—almost—threatening when youth scorns age and two old men offer to defend themselves against the fancy swordplay and vigour of a 'boy', but common sense and Don Pedro's authority prevail. The brothers withdraw, and the impassioned verse yields to conversational prose when Benedick enters the scene.

Don Pedro and Claudio persist in their light-hearted raillery, oblivious to the growing anger with which Benedick hears their jests, and, desperately trying to engage him in their mirth, they almost betray the trick which brought him to love Beatrice. Not until he discharges himself from the company of Don Pedro, asserting Hero's innocence and Don John's guilt, does Benedick begin to persuade them to take him seriously. The truth is slow to dawn on Don Pedro (and slower still on Claudio), and the arrival of Dogberry with his prisoners causes even more suspenseful, this time comic, delay. But Borachio's confession, a simple statement of facts that attempts no excuses, makes all plain.

Verse returns to express the emotion of Claudio's recognition and the caustic irony of Leonato's indictment—although this soon changes to forgiveness as he prepares the way for the final deception with his brother's pretended daughter who 'alone is heir to both of us': Claudio may be reassured even on the matter of inheritance. Borachio also reaches to the dignity of verse when he generously exonerates Margaret from all blame, but Dogberry brings everything back to prose and laughter as, rewarded for his pains, he bows out of the play in a fluster of malapropisms: 'if a merry meeting may be wished, God prohibit it'.

Scene 2   In a happy interlude, Benedick makes a valiant attempt to compose a poem for Beatrice. Poetic language does not come easily to him— 'I was not born under a rhyming planet'—and he is more comfortable, when Beatrice comes to him, to resume their former badinage, recognizing that they are both 'too wise to love peaceably'. Hours pass quickly in their teasing company . . .

Scene 3   . . . and soon it is time for Claudio to perform his act of penitence at Hero's tomb, accompanied by Don Pedro and as many attendants, 'with tapers, all wearing mourning', as Shakespeare's dramatic company could supply to create a solemn atmosphere. Although it is short, the scene must have enough intensity to suggest genuine remorse and sorrow in the gloom of night—which is dispersed by Don Pedro's aubade:

> Good morning, masters, put your torches out.
>   The wolves have prey'd, and look, the gentle day
> Before the wheels of Phoebus round about
>   Dapples the drowsy east with spots of grey.

A new day is dawning, and a regenerate Claudio, sharing the rhymes, can now prepare to meet a restored Hero.

Scene 4   A 'fair assembly' is gathering. Leonato, fully convinced of Hero's innocence, absolves Don Pedro and Claudio ('although Margaret was in some fault for this'), and receives them back into favour. Benedick, slightly embarrassed, prepares to make it a double wedding, and Claudio, eager to make amends, seems ready to 'seize upon' any of the masked ladies. Antonio repeats the simple ceremony from the ballroom scene (*2*, 1, 299–301), and 'Another Hero' stands revealed! Beatrice and Benedick, their own deception uncovered and their bickering silenced in a kiss, agree together, and Benedick, urging Don Pedro to follow his example (because there is 'no staff more reverend than one tipped with horn'), leads the full company off into a final dance.

The Outsider

Messina is a world where everyone *talks*! Skill with words is essential for social survival, and a delight in language is shared by courtiers and constabulary alike. But Don John cannot join in: 'I am not of many words.' He reserves his angry self-mockery for the intimacy of his conversations with Conrad and Borachio, and knows that he is permanently excluded from the family togetherness that is celebrated in Leonato's 'great supper': 'Their cheer is the greater that I am subdued.'

Don John has been defeated: he had 'stood out' against his brother, his defiance failed, and the disgrace is bitter to him—and made worse by his captive condition, 'trusted with a muzzle, and enfranchised with a clog'. The other characters look on him warily. Leonato's hospitality is conditional upon Don John's being reconciled with his brother; Beatrice claims to have indigestion—heartburn—whenever she sees him; and even the gentle Hero can diagnose 'a very melancholy disposition'. But there is still more to account for his isolation.

Shakespeare needed a villain who would take the place of the jealous rival of the source story of *Much Ado About Nothing* (see 'Source, Text, and Date', p.xxvi), and he found one ready-made in popular theories about psychological types: 'Bastards are envious: for he that cannot possibly mend his case will do what he can to impair others'.[1] Although Shakespeare gives Don John some reason for hating Claudio ('that young start-up hath all the glory of my overthrow'), the type figure of 'The Bastard' needed—for the Elizabethans—no further motivation for wickedness beyond the illegitimacy that barred him from the inheritance and respect enjoyed by his legitimate brother. And the presence of such a character stands as a constant threat to the stability of a society which is grounded in the sanctity of marriage, where family values are of the essence, and where the joyful tears of Claudio's uncle are seen as 'A kind overflow of kindness'.

'*Enter . . . Don John the Bastard*': the description in this stage direction must be a prompt for his memory as Shakespeare is writing the play, but perhaps sixteenth and seventeenth century audiences (without theatre programmes or cast lists) would have

[1] Francis Bacon, 'Of Envy' (*Essays*, 1625).

been able somehow to deduce the character's illegitimacy from his appearance—possibly even bearing the 'bend sinister' (a diagonal band from left to right) on his military standard as he makes his way home from the battle. Apart from the stage directions, however, there is no reference to Don John's birth in the text of the play until Benedick, defending his friends even though he has deserted them, lays the blame for Hero's betrayal where it belongs. All three of the noblemen joined in the denunciation of Hero, he says, but

> Two of them have the very bent of honour,
> And if their wisdoms be misled in this
> The practice of it lives in John the Bastard,
> Whose spirits toil in frame of villainies.   (4, 1, 186–9)

Don John vanishes from Messina after the cruelty of the church scene and, although we hear in the very last lines of the play that he has been arrested, we are no longer interested in his fate. The evil he represented has been banished, and the 'brave punishments' that Benedick promises can wait until tomorrow: today is for dancing—'love's proper exercise'.[2]

Shakespeare's plays have two other memorable 'Bastards'—Philip Falconbridge in *King John*, and Edmund, the bastard son of Gloucester in *King Lear*. As if to justify his villainy, Edmund gives a most articulate—even sympathetic—statement of his 'case':

> Why bastard? Wherefore base?
> When my dimensions are as well compact,
> My mind as generous, and my shape as true
> As honest madam's issue? Why brand they us
> With base? with baseness? bastardy? base, base?
> Who in the lusty stealth of nature take
> More composition and fierce quality
> Than doth, within a dull, stale, tired bed,
> Go to th'creating a whole tribe of fops
> Got 'tween asleep and wake?   (1, 2, 6–15)

His words express the popular Elizabethan belief in the superior physical and intellectual energy of the illegitimate child—qualities Shakespeare had already demonstrated in Philip the Bastard, who

---

[2] Sir John Davies, *Orchestra, or a Poem of Dancing* (1596, stanza 18):
   This wondrous miracle did Love devise,
   For dancing is love's proper exercise.

asserts that if he looked like his brother, Robert Falconbridge—

> And if my legs were two such riding-rods
> My arms such eel-skins stuff'd, my face so thin
> That in mine ear I durst not stick a rose
> Lest men should say 'Look, where three-farthings
>   goes!'
> And, to his shape, were heir to all this land (*1*, 1, 140–4)

—he would rather be the man he is, full of life and energy.

Shakespeare's Style

Much Ado About Nothing, unlike most of Shakespeare's plays, is written largely in prose—a highly skilled, witty prose which seems to spring spontaneously from the character's imagination, and which is a great delight for the actors who speak it. Images are generated apparently through free association, and tossed from one speaker to another, caught and developed before being passed on again. The language can be colloquial or formal (but is almost always courteous), and changes from the learned to the familiar even within a phrase. This is perfect for the comedy scenes, where two or more characters, at ease with themselves and their companion[s], compete to be the most entertaining:

> **Benedick**
> I have almost matter enough in me for such an embassage. And so I commit you—
>
> **Claudio**
> To the tuition of God. From my house, if I had it—
>
> **Don Pedro**
> The sixth of July, your loving friend, Benedick.
>
> **Benedick**
> Nay, mock not, mock not. The body of your discourse is sometime guarded with fragments, and the guards are but slightly basted on neither. Ere you flout old ends any further, examine your conscience. And so I leave you.

Benedick's irony magnifies Don Pedro's little errand into an 'embassage', but the formality of his leave taking is turned against him when Claudio seizes on his 'commit' and, backed by Don Pedro, develops it into a conventional letter-ending. Benedick, rebuking the mockery, juggles with the terms of another idea whose relevance (although of course the end is implicit in the beginning) is not obvious until he has finished and revealed the pun on 'ends'—the endings of letters, and the leftover scraps of fabric that a tailor would use to trim a garment.

Although prose is sufficient for most occasions, verse has an even greater range and flexibility when the subject is delicate or deeply felt, or when the speaker is of high degree or serious in intent. In *Much Ado*, the romantic (and near-tragic) love affair of Claudio and Hero is conducted in sympathetic blank verse, the form in which most of Shakespeare's plays and those of his contemporaries are written. It is a very flexible medium, capable— like the human speaking voice—of a wide range of tones. Basically the lines, called 'iambic pentameters', are unrhymed and have ten syllables with alternating stresses (just like normal English speech) which divide them into five 'feet'. The rhythm of the pentameter is initiated in the first scene of the play when Claudio takes Don Pedro into his confidence—

Claudio
My liége, your híghness nów may dó me góod.

Don Pedro
My lóve is thíne to téach. Teach ít but hów
And thóu shalt sée how ápt it ís to léarn
Aný hard lésson thát may dó thee góod.

Claudio
Hath Léonáto ány són, my lórd?

Don Pedro
No chíld but Héro. Shé's his ónly héir.
Dost thóu afféct her, Cláudio?

Claudio
                Ó my lórd,
When yóu went ónward ón this énded áction
I lóok'd upón her wíth a sóldier's éye,
That lík'd, but hád a róugher tásk in hánd
Than tó drive líking tó the náme of lóve.
But nów I ám retúrn'd, and thát war-thóughts
Have léft their pláces vácant, ín their róoms
Come thrónging sóft and délicáte desíres,
All prómpting mé how fáir young Héro ís,
Saýing I lík'd her ére I wént to wárs.   (*1*, 1, 268–94)

At the beginning of his career Shakespeare wrote regular, 'end-stopped', lines in which the unit of meaning was contained within the pentameter (as in the last line of this quotation), but now he is well in control of his medium, and in *Much Ado About Nothing* the verse is smooth and silky, and the sense flows easily between the lines, only curbed by a gentle mid-line pause (a 'caesura'). Two (or more) speakers may share a line, whether they are in agreement or at odds with each other, and this makes for a natural and speedy delivery.

Easily the best way to understand and appreciate Shakespeare's verse is to read it aloud! Don't be captivated by the dominant rhythm, but decide which are the most important words in each line and use the regular metre to drive them forward to the listeners.

Source, Text, and Date

Shakespeare found many versions of the story of Claudio and Hero, but his main source for the play was a tale by Matteo Bandello which was published in 1554 and which his knowledge of Latin would have enabled him to read in the original Italian.

It is a tale of love and friendship—male friendship. Sir Timbreo, a rich courtier and a favourite of the King of Aragon, falls in love with Fenicia, the daughter of a nobleman of Messina, and a marriage is arranged through the marriage-broker. But a scheme to prevent this is devised by Timbreo's friend Girondo, who is himself in love with the girl. Timbreo is brought to witness an unknown man climbing a ladder into Fenicia's house, and his immediate reaction (still acting through an intermediary) is to cancel the wedding plans. On hearing the bad news, Fenicia falls into a swoon and is believed to be dead. When she revives she is sent away into the country by her father—who never doubts his daughter's innocence but thinks that there are financial reasons for Timbreo's rejection of her. A mock funeral is held, and an empty coffin placed in the family vault. Timbreo, who has begun to appreciate the flimsiness of his evidence, is overcome with remorse, Girondo confesses everything, and both men ask Fenicia's father for his forgiveness. A second bride, said to be Fenicia's even more beautiful sister, is married to Timbreo and proves (of course) to be Fenicia herself—whose real sister stands ready to become the wife of Girondo, now fully reconciled with Timbreo.

Shakespeare pays little attention to the 'love-versus-friendship' aspect of this story—perhaps because in earlier plays (such as *Two Gentlemen of Verona*) he had found its conventions to be artificial and unconvincing. Instead he develops Claudio's friend into the character of Benedick, giving him his own scenario and dilemma with Beatrice, a personality entirely of Shakespeare's creation.

A single Quarto, published in 1600, gives the authoritative text for *Much Ado About Nothing*. This seems to have been printed from Shakespeare's own manuscript (not from a theatrical copy), and shows the dramatist still at work, leaving some loose ends and several lines that are neither verse nor prose, as well as stage directions and speech prefixes that are sometimes uncertain or irregular—and sometimes unusually informative. Directions and speech prefixes identifying Dogberry as 'Ke' and 'Andrew' (i.e. 'Merry Andrew', the generic name for the stage buffoon) show Shakespeare designing the character on and for the company's leading comic actor, Will Kemp. The prefix 'Cowley' for Verges points to another comedian, Richard Cowley, whose spindly frame and pale complexion would contrast with Kemp's burly agility.

The present edition makes use of thc text established by Sheldon P. Zitner in 1993 for the Oxford Shakespeare (World's Classics).

The play is not mentioned in *Palladis Tamia*, Francis Meres's list of the best contemporary English writing, which was entered for publication in the Stationers' Register in September 1598, but the date of composition cannot have been much later than this, since Will Kemp had left the company, the Lord Chamberlain's Men, when he started a much-publicized jig from London to Norwich on 11 February 1599.

People in the Play

Don Pedro	*Prince of Aragon*
Don John	*his illegitimate brother*
Claudio	*a young lord of Florence*
Benedick	*a young lord of Padua*
Conrad	*followers of* Don John
Borachio	
Balthasar	*a singer, attendant upon* Don Pedro

Leonato	*Governor of Messina*
Antonio	*his brother*
Hero	Leonato*'s daughter*
Beatrice	Leonato*'s niece*
Margaret	*Gentlewomen attending upon* Hero
Ursula	

Friar Francis	*a priest*
Dogberry	*master constable*
Verges	*headborough,* Dogberry*'s assistant*

Watchmen, a Sexton, a lord, messengers

Most of the action takes place outside, inside, and around the house and garden of Leonato, *Governor of Messina*

Act I

Act I   Scene I

Leonato welcomes Don Pedro to his house.
Beatrice engages with Benedick in a battle of
wits, Claudio declares his love for Hero, and
Don Pedro proposes a stratagem.

3 *three leagues*: i.e. about nine miles, or
fourteen kilometres.

5 *action*: battle.

6 *sort*: rank.
   none of name: no one you would know,
   no one important.

11 *equally remembered*: properly rewarded.

17 *an uncle*: The uncle is never mentioned
again.

Scene I

Enter Leonato, *governor of Messina,* Hero
his daughter, and Beatrice *his niece, with a*
Messenger

Leonato
I learn in this letter that Don Pedro of Aragon comes
this night to Messina.

Messenger
He is very near by this. He was not three leagues off
when I left him.

Leonato
5 How many gentlemen have you lost in this action?

Messenger
But few of any sort, and none of name.

Leonato
A victory is twice itself when the achiever brings
home full numbers. I find here that Don Pedro hath
bestowed much honour on a young Florentine called
10 Claudio.

Messenger
Much deserved on his part, and equally remembered
by Don Pedro. He hath borne himself beyond the
promise of his age, doing in the figure of a lamb the
feats of a lion. He hath indeed better bettered
15 expectation than you must expect of me to tell you
how.

Leonato
He hath an uncle here in Messina will be very much
glad of it.

Messenger
I have already delivered him letters, and there
20 appears much joy in him, even so much that joy

21 *modest*: moderate.

21–2 *a badge of bitterness*: i.e. a tear, the sign of grief; badges worn by servants indicated their status and their master's rank. The Messenger's elaborate formality confuses Leonato for a moment.

25 *kind . . . kindness*: Leonato attempts a feeble pun on the different senses of 'kind' (= generous, natural, humane, or kinship).

28 *Montanto*: Beatrice coins the name (with obvious sexual innuendo) from a fencing term for an upward thrust.

31 *sort*: rank.

34 *pleasant*: amusing.

35 *bills*: advertisements.
36 *at the flight*: to an archery competition: Benedick has claimed to be a better lady-killer than Cupid.
37 *subscribed for*: responded on behalf of.
38 *bird-bolt*: blunt wooden-headed arrow used for stunning birds (given to children and fools).

41 *tax*: criticize.
42 *be meet*: get even.

44 *holp*: helped.
45 *valiant trencherman*: hearty eater.
46 *stomach*: appetite, courage.

48 *to a lord*: compared to, faced with.

could not show itself modest enough without a badge of bitterness.

Leonato
Did he break out into tears?

Messenger
In great measure.

Leonato
25 A kind overflow of kindness; there are no faces truer than those that are so washed. How much better is it to weep at joy than to joy at weeping!

Beatrice
I pray you, is Signor Montanto returned from the wars, or no?

Messenger
30 I know none of that name, lady. There was none such in the army, of any sort.

Leonato
What is he that you ask for, niece?

Hero
My cousin means Signor Benedick of Padua.

Messenger
O, he's returned, and as pleasant as ever he was.

Beatrice
35 He set up his bills here in Messina, and challenged Cupid at the flight; and my uncle's fool, reading the challenge, subscribed for Cupid and challenged him at the bird-bolt. I pray you, how many hath he killed and eaten in these wars? But how many hath he
40 killed? For indeed I promised to eat all of his killing.

Leonato
Faith, niece, you tax Signor Benedick too much. But he'll be meet with you, I doubt it not.

Messenger
He hath done good service, lady, in these wars.

Beatrice
You had musty victual, and he hath holp to eat it. He
45 is a very valiant trencherman; he hath an excellent stomach.

Messenger
And a good soldier too, lady.

Beatrice
And a good soldier to a lady, but what is he to a lord?

49 *stuffed with*: full of.

51 *stuffed man*: i.e. scarecrow.

58 *five wits*: Philosophers distinguished five separate mental faculties: imagination, fancy, judgement, memory, and common sense (which moderated all the others).

60–1 *for a difference*: as a heraldic mark indicating the junior branch of the family (the horse here would be the senior and superior).

62–3 *reasonable creature*: The capacity for reason is what differentiates man from all other animals.

63 *companion*: mate.

66 *faith*: i.e. the faith he has just sworn to his latest 'brother'.

67 *ever*: always.

67–8 *next block*: newest mould.

69 *books*: good books, favour.

70 *An*: if.
   study: library.

72 *squarer*: hooligan.

78 *presently*: immediately.

80 *a*: he.

Messenger
A lord to a lord, a man to a man, stuffed with all
50 honourable virtues.
   Beatrice
It is so, indeed. He is no less than a stuffed man. But
for the stuffing—well, we are all mortal.
   Leonato
You must not, sir, mistake my niece. There is a kind
of merry war betwixt Signor Benedick and her. They
55 never meet but there's a skirmish of wit between
them.
   Beatrice
Alas, he gets nothing by that. In our last conflict four
of his five wits went halting off, and now is the whole
man governed with one; so that if he have wit
60 enough to keep himself warm, let him bear it for a
difference between himself and his horse, for it is all
the wealth that he hath left to be known a reasonable
creature. Who is his companion now? He hath every
month a new sworn brother.
   Messenger
65 Is't possible?
   Beatrice
Very easily possible. He wears his faith but as the
fashion of his hat; it ever changes with the next
block.
   Messenger
I see, lady, the gentleman is not in your books.
   Beatrice
70 No. An he were, I would burn my study. But I pray
you, who is his companion? Is there no young
squarer now that will make a voyage with him to the
devil?
   Messenger
He is most in the company of the right noble
75 Claudio.
   Beatrice
O Lord, he will hang upon him like a disease. He is
sooner caught than the pestilence, and the taker runs
presently mad. God help the noble Claudio. If he
have caught the Benedick, it will cost him a thousand
80 pound ere a be cured.

Messenger
I will hold friends with you, lady.
Beatrice
Do, good friend.
Leonato
You will never run mad, niece.
Beatrice
No, not till a hot January.
Messenger
85 Don Pedro is approached.

Enter Don Pedro, Claudio, Benedick,
Balthasar, *and* Don John *the Bastard*

Don Pedro
Good Signor Leonato, are you come to meet your
trouble? The fashion of the world is to avoid cost,
and you encounter it.
Leonato
Never came trouble to my house in the likeness of
90 your grace; for trouble being gone, comfort should
remain. But when you depart from me, sorrow
abides and happiness takes his leave.
Don Pedro
You embrace your charge too willingly. I think this is
your daughter.
Leonato
95 Her mother hath many times told me so.
Benedick
Were you in doubt, sir, that you asked her?
Leonato
Signor Benedick, no, for then were you a child.
Don Pedro
You have it full, Benedick. We may guess by this
what you are, being a man. Truly, the lady fathers
100 herself. Be happy, lady, for you are like an
honourable father.

Speaks privately with Leonato

Benedick
If Signor Leonato be her father, she would not have
his head on her shoulders for all Messina, as like him
as she is.

85   *is approached*: is approaching.
85s.d. *the Bastard*: The description shows
Shakespeare's first conception of this
character—the text of the play makes
no reference to Don John's illegitimacy
until *4, 1, 187* (see 'The Outsider',
p.xx).

99   *what you are*: i.e. a womanizer.
99–100 *fathers herself*: i.e. in her
resemblance to Leonato.

103   *his head*: i.e. because he is bearded and
has grey hair.

Beatrice

105 I wonder that you will still be talking, Signor
Benedick; nobody marks you.

Benedick

What, my dear Lady Disdain! Are you yet living?

Beatrice

Is it possible disdain should die while she hath such
meet food to feed it as Signor Benedick? Courtesy
110 itself must convert to disdain if you come in her
presence.

Benedick

Then is courtesy a turncoat. But it is certain I am
loved of all ladies, only you excepted. And I would I
could find in my heart that I had not a hard heart,
115 for truly I love none.

Beatrice

A dear happiness to women. They would else have
been troubled with a pernicious suitor. I thank God
and my cold blood I am of your humour for that. I
had rather hear my dog bark at a crow than a man
120 swear he loves me.

Benedick

God keep your ladyship still in that mind. So some
gentleman or other shall scape a predestinate
scratched face.

Beatrice

Scratching could not make it worse an 'twere such a
125 face as yours were.

Benedick

Well, you are a rare parrot-teacher.

Beatrice

A bird of my tongue is better than a beast of yours.

Benedick

I would my horse had the speed of your tongue, and
so good a continuer. But keep your way, o' God's
130 name. I have done.

Beatrice

You always end with a jade's trick. I know you of old.

Don Pedro

[*Ending his talk with* Leonato] That is the sum of all,
Leonato.—Signor Claudio and Signor Benedick, my
dear friend Leonato hath invited you all. I tell him

109 *meet*: appropriate (and with a pun on
'meat').

116 *dear happiness*: precious piece of luck.

118 *of your . . . that*: of your frame of mind
on that point.

127 *A bird . . . yours*: i.e. 'My talking bird is
better than your dumb beast.'
128–9 *I would . . . continuer*: 'I wish my horse
went as fast as your tongue and could
go on so long.'
131 *with . . . trick*: i.e. like a stubborn horse
refusing to go on.

135 we shall stay here at the least a month, and he
heartily prays some occasion may detain us longer. I
dare swear he is no hypocrite, but prays from his
heart.

Leonato

If you swear, my lord, you shall not be forsworn. [*To*
140 Don John] Let me bid you welcome, my lord. Being
reconciled to the prince your brother, I owe you all
duty.

Don John

I thank you. I am not of many words, but I thank
you.

Leonato

145 [*To* Don Pedro] Please it your grace lead on?

Don Pedro

Your hand, Leonato. We will go together.

[*Exeunt all but* Benedick *and* Claudio

Claudio

Benedick, didst thou note the daughter of Signor
Leonato?

Benedick

I noted her not, but I looked on her.

Claudio

150 Is she not a modest young lady?

Benedick

Do you question me as an honest man should do, for
my simple true judgement, or would you have me
speak after my custom, as being a professed tyrant to
their sex?

Claudio

155 No, I pray thee speak in sober judgement.

Benedick

Why, i' faith, methinks she's too low for a high
praise, too brown for a fair praise, and too little for a
great praise. Only this commendation I can afford
her, that were she other than she is she were
160 unhandsome, and being no other but as she is, I do
not like her.

Claudio

Thou thinkest I am in sport. I pray thee tell me truly
how thou likest her.

---

140 *Being*: since you are.

149 *noted her not*: paid no special attention
to her.

153 *after my custom*: Benedick admits that
his misogyny is not entirely serious.
professed: declared.

156 *low*: short.

Benedick

Would you buy her, that you enquire after her?

Claudio

165 Can the world buy such a jewel?

Benedick

Yea, and a case to put it into. But speak you this with a sad brow, or do you play the flouting Jack, to tell us Cupid is a good hare-finder and Vulcan a rare carpenter? Come, in what key shall a man take you
170 to go in the song?

Claudio

In mine eye she is the sweetest lady that ever I looked on.

Benedick

I can see yet without spectacles, and I see no such matter. There's her cousin, an she were not
175 possessed with a fury, exceeds her as much in beauty as the first of May doth the last of December. But I hope you have no intent to turn husband, have you?

Claudio

I would scarce trust myself though I had sworn the contrary, if Hero would be my wife.

Benedick

180 Is't come to this? In faith, hath not the world one man but he will wear his cap with suspicion? Shall I never see a bachelor of three-score again? Go to, i' faith, an thou wilt needs thrust thy neck into a yoke, wear the print of it, and sigh away Sundays. Look,
185 Don Pedro is returned to seek you.

167 *sad*: serious.
  flouting Jack: scornful fellow.
168–9 *Cupid . . . carpenter*: Cupid in fact was blind, and Vulcan was a blacksmith.
169–70 *key . . . song*: musical key to sing with you, mood to understand you.

174 *cousin*: The word was used loosely for any family connection; the exact relationship between Beatrice and Hero is never explained.
  an: if.

181 *wear . . . suspicion*: wear a cap because he suspects his head has sprouted the horns of a cuckold (= the husband of an unfaithful wife).
184 *sigh away Sundays*: i.e. because he cannot go out with his male companions.

Enter Don Pedro

Don Pedro
What secret hath held you here that you followed not
to Leonato's?

Benedick
I would your grace would constrain me to tell.

Don Pedro
I charge thee on thy allegiance.

Benedick
190 You hear, Count Claudio? I can be secret as a dumb
man; I would have you think so. But on my
allegiance, mark you this—on my allegiance—he is
in love! With who? Now that is your grace's part.
Mark how short his answer is—with Hero, Leonato's
195 short daughter.

Claudio
If this were so, so were it uttered.

Benedick
Like the old tale, my lord: 'It is not so, nor 'twas not
so, but indeed, God forbid it should be so.'

Claudio
If my passion change not shortly, God forbid it
200 should be otherwise.

Don Pedro
Amen, if you love her, for the lady is very well
worthy.

Claudio
You speak this to fetch me in, my lord.

Don Pedro
By my troth, I speak my thought.

Claudio
205 And in faith, my lord, I spoke mine.

Benedick
And by my two faiths and troths, my lord, I spoke
mine.

Claudio
That I love her, I feel.

Don Pedro
That she is worthy, I know.

188 *would*: wish.

189 *charge . . . allegiance*: Benedick's sworn
allegiance to Don Pedro would override
other loyalties.

197 *old tale*: Benedick refers to a folktale of
a robber-bridegroom whose crimes were
discovered by his bride.

203 *fetch me in*: trick me into a confession.

206 *my two . . . troths*: dual loyalties—to
Don Pedro and to Claudio.

213–14 *heretic . . . beauty*: The conventions of courtly love became a 'religion' which demanded that all its adherents should at all times honour and serve the beauty of their ladies.

215 *maintain his part*: argue his position (with sexual innuendo).

215–16 *in . . . will*: through stubborn determination.

219–20 *I will . . . baldric*: 'I will wear in my forehead a horn for summoning hounds, or hang my hunting-horn in an invisible belt'—i.e. 'risk being known as a cuckold, or try to hide the fact that I have been cuckolded'.

223 *fine*: conclusion.

225 *pale with love*: Sighs of love were said to deplete the blood.

229 *ballad*: Most ballads—then as now—were about love.

234 *hang . . . cat*: A cat suspended in a leather bottle or basket was sometimes used as a target for archery practice.

236 *called Adam*: Adam Bell was a famous archer.

Benedick

210 That I neither feel how she should be loved nor know how she should be worthy is the opinion that fire cannot melt out of me. I will die in it at the stake.

Don Pedro

Thou wast ever an obstinate heretic in the despite of beauty.

Claudio

215 And never could maintain his part but in the force of his will.

Benedick

That a woman conceived me, I thank her. That she brought me up, I likewise give her most humble thanks. But that I will have a recheat winded in my

220 forehead, or hang my bugle in an invisible baldric, all women shall pardon me. Because I will not do them the wrong to mistrust any, I will do myself the right to trust none. And the fine is—for the which I may go the finer—I will live a bachelor.

Don Pedro

225 I shall see thee ere I die look pale with love.

Benedick

With anger, with sickness, or with hunger, my lord; not with love. Prove that ever I lose more blood with love than I will get again with drinking, pick out mine eyes with a ballad-maker's pen and hang me up

230 at the door of a brothel house for the sign of blind Cupid.

Don Pedro

Well, if ever thou dost fall from this faith thou wilt prove a notable argument.

Benedick

If I do, hang me in a bottle like a cat, and shoot at

235 me, and he that hits me, let him be clapped on the shoulder and called Adam.

Don Pedro

Well, as time shall try. 'In time the savage bull doth bear the yoke.'

Benedick

The savage bull may, but if ever the sensible

240 Benedick bear it, pluck off the bull's horns and set them in my forehead, and let me be vilely painted, and in such great letters as they write 'Here is good

245–6 *horn-mad*: mad as a charging bull (with the obvious allusion to the cuckold's horns).

247 *spent . . . quiver*: used up all his arrows.
Venice: The city was renowned (in Elizabethan England) for sexual licence.

250 *temporize . . . hours*: weaken as time goes by.

255 *matter*: understanding.

256 *I commit you*: Benedick parodies the formal closing of a letter.

257 *tuition*: safe-keeping.
From my house: i.e. the address from which he is writing.

259 *body*: substance, basic fabric (Benedick's imagery is from tailoring).

260 *guarded*: decorated.

261 *basted on*: loosely tacked on.

262 *flout*: scoff at.
ends: tags, quotations.

264 *My liege . . . good*: Changing the mood and subject, Claudio shifts the scene into blank verse.

268 *any son*: i.e. an heir.

270 *affect*: love.

horse to hire', let them signify under my sign 'Here you may see Benedick, the married man.'

Claudio

245 If this should ever happen thou wouldst be horn-mad.

Don Pedro

Nay, if Cupid have not spent all his quiver in Venice, thou wilt quake for this shortly.

Benedick

I look for an earthquake too, then.

Don Pedro

250 Well, you will temporize with the hours. In the meantime, good Signor Benedick, repair to Leonato's. Commend me to him, and tell him I will not fail him at supper, for indeed he hath made great preparation.

Benedick

255 I have almost matter enough in me for such an embassage. And so I commit you—

Claudio

To the tuition of God. From my house, if I had it—

Don Pedro

The sixth of July, your loving friend, Benedick.

Benedick

Nay, mock not, mock not. The body of your
260 discourse is sometime guarded with fragments, and the guards are but slightly basted on neither. Ere you flout old ends any further, examine your conscience. And so I leave you.   [*Exit*

Claudio

My liege, your highness now may do me good.

Don Pedro

265 My love is thine to teach. Teach it but how
And thou shalt see how apt it is to learn
Any hard lesson that may do thee good.

Claudio

Hath Leonato any son, my lord?

Don Pedro

No child but Hero. She's his only heir.

270 Dost thou affect her, Claudio?

Claudio

O my lord,
When you went onward on this ended action
I look'd upon her with a soldier's eye,
That lik'd, but had a rougher task in hand
Than to drive liking to the name of love.
275 But now I am return'd, and that war-thoughts
Have left their places vacant, in their rooms
Come thronging soft and delicate desires,
All prompting me how fair young Hero is,
Saying I lik'd her ere I went to wars.

Don Pedro
280 Thou wilt be like a lover presently,
And tire the hearer with a book of words.
If thou dost love fair Hero, cherish it,
And I will break with her and with her father,
And thou shalt have her. Was't not to this end
285 That thou began'st to twist so fine a story?

Claudio
How sweetly you do minister to love
That know love's grief by his complexion.
But lest my liking might too sudden seem,
I would have salv'd it with a longer treatise.

Don Pedro
290 What need the bridge much broader than the flood?
The fairest grant is the necessity.
Look what will serve is fit. 'Tis once. Thou lovest,
And I will fit thee with the remedy.
I know we shall have revelling tonight.
295 I will assume thy part in some disguise,
And tell fair Hero I am Claudio.
And in her bosom I'll unclasp my heart
And take her hearing prisoner with the force
And strong encounter of my amorous tale.
300 Then after to her father will I break,
And the conclusion is, she shall be thine.
In practice let us put it presently. [*Exeunt*

281 *book of words*: collection of love poems (conventionally required of lovers).

283 *break with*: raise the matter with.

287 *complexion*: appearance.

289 *I would . . . treatise*: 'I wanted to give a fuller account of it.'

290 *flood*: river.

291 *The . . . necessity*: 'The best gift is the one you want.'

292 *Look what*: whatever.
once: enough.

297 *in her bosom*: privately.
unclasp: open; fine books were often fastened with clasps.

Act 1   Scene 2

The first mistake: Leonato is told that Don
Pedro will woo Hero for himself.

1 *my cousin*: This cousin is never
   mentioned again in the play.

6 *As . . . them*: 'as time will tell'.
8 *Thick-pleached alley*: path hedged in by
   closely interwoven branches.

10 *discovered*: revealed.
13 *accordant*: in agreement.

13–14 *take . . . top*: seize the opportunity
   (an allusion to the proverb 'Take
   Occasion by the forelock, for she is bald
   behind').

Scene 2

> *Enter* Leonato, *meeting old* Antonio, *his*
> *brother*

Leonato
How now, brother, where is my cousin, your son?
Hath he provided this music?

Antonio
He is very busy about it. But brother, I can tell you
strange news that you yet dreamt not of.

Leonato
5 Are they good?

Antonio
As the event stamps them. But they have a good
cover; they show well outward. The prince and
Count Claudio, walking in a thick-pleached alley in
mine orchard, were thus much overheard by a man
10 of mine: the prince discovered to Claudio that he
loved my niece, your daughter, and meant to
acknowledge it this night in a dance and, if he found
her accordant, he meant to take the present time by
the top and instantly break with you of it.

Leonato
15 Hath the fellow any wit that told you this?

Antonio

A good sharp fellow. I will send for him, and question him yourself.

Leonato

No, no. We will hold it as a dream till it appear itself. But I will acquaint my daughter withal, that she may
20 be the better prepared for an answer if peradventure this be true. Go you and tell her of it.

Enter Attendants

Cousins, you know what you have to do.—O, I cry you mercy, friend. Go you with me and I will use your skill.—Good cousin, have a care this busy time.

[*Exeunt*

1 *What the goodyear*: Conrad uses a mild oath.

2 *measure*: proportion.

7 *sufferance*: endurance.

9 *born under Saturn*: The planet was believed to have a malign influence.

10 *mortifying mischief*: shameful disgrace (i.e. his defeat by Don Pedro, present captivity—and also, perhaps, illegitimate birth).

15 *claw . . . humour*: pander to nobody's fancy.

Scene 3

Enter Don John *the Bastard and* Conrad,
his companion

Conrad

What the goodyear, my lord. Why are you thus out of measure sad?

Don John

There is no measure in the occasion that breeds it; therefore the sadness is without limit.

Conrad

5 You should hear reason.

Don John

And when I have heard it, what blessing brings it?

Conrad

If not a present remedy, at least a patient sufferance.

Don John

I wonder that thou, being—as thou say'st thou art—born under Saturn, goest about to apply a moral
10 medicine to a mortifying mischief. I cannot hide what I am. I must be sad when I have cause, and smile at no man's jests; eat when I have stomach, and wait for no man's leisure; sleep when I am drowsy, and tend on no man's business; laugh when
15 I am merry, and claw no man in his humour.

Conrad

Yea, but you must not make the full show of this till you may do it without controlment. You have of late stood out against your brother, and he hath ta'en you newly into his grace, where it is impossible you
20 should take true root but by the fair weather that you make yourself. It is needful that you frame the season for your own harvest.

Don John

I had rather be a canker in a hedge than a rose in his grace. And it better fits my blood to be disdained of
25 all than to fashion a carriage to rob love from any. In this, though I cannot be said to be a flattering honest man, it must not be denied but I am a plain-dealing villain. I am trusted with a muzzle, and enfranchised with a clog. Therefore I have decreed not to sing in
30 my cage. If I had my mouth I would bite. If I had my liberty I would do my liking. In the meantime, let me be that I am, and seek not to alter me.

Conrad

Can you make no use of your discontent?

Don John

I make all use of it, for I use it only. Who comes
35 here?

Enter Borachio

What news, Borachio?

Borachio

I came yonder from a great supper. The prince your brother is royally entertained by Leonato, and I can give you intelligence of an intended marriage.

Don John

40 Will it serve for any model to build mischief on? What is he for a fool that betroths himself to unquietness?

Borachio

Marry, it is your brother's right hand.

Don John

Who, the most exquisite Claudio?

Borachio

45 Even he.

20 *fair weather*: favourable opportunities.

23 *canker*: dog-rose, wild rose—*also* evil, diseased growth.
24 *blood*: temperament, [illegitimate] birth.
25 *fashion a carriage*: pretend a manner.
28–9 *enfranchised . . . clog*: set free with a weight fastened on my leg.

34 *use it only*: am *always* discontented.
36 *Borachio*: The name is from the Spanish for 'wine-bottle'.
39 *intelligence*: information.
40 *model*: ground-plan (architectural).

46 *proper squire*: fine young gentleman
(Don John is contemptuous).

49 *forward*: precocious.
March chick: bird hatched very early.

50 *entertained for*: hired as.
perfumer: The Elizabethans used
aromatic herbs as air-fresheners.

51 *comes me*: along comes; 'me' here is a
so-called 'ethical dative', which
functions only to intensify the verb.

53 *arras*: decorative tapestry hung before
the wall, providing insulation—and a
hiding-place; perhaps the conversation
has been repeated (see *1, 2, 8note*), or
perhaps Shakespeare has forgotten its
location.

58 *cross*: frustrate, impede.

59 *bless*: i.e. by making the sign of the
cross.
sure: safe, loyal.

63 *subdued*: depressed *and* suppressed.

63–4 *o' my mind*: had the same—probably
poisonous—thoughts as I have.

64 *prove*: find out.

Don John

A proper squire. And who, and who? Which way
looks he?

Borachio

Marry, on Hero, the daughter and heir of Leonato.

Don John

A very forward March chick. How came you to this?

Borachio

50 Being entertained for a perfumer, as I was smoking a
musty room, comes me the prince and Claudio,
hand in hand, in sad conference. I whipped me
behind the arras, and there heard it agreed upon that
the prince should woo Hero for himself and, having

55 obtained her, give her to Count Claudio.

Don John

Come, come, let us thither. This may prove food to
my displeasure. That young start-up hath all the
glory of my overthrow. If I can cross him any way, I
bless myself every way. You are both sure, and will

60 assist me?

Conrad

To the death, my lord.

Don John

Let us to the great supper. Their cheer is the greater
that I am subdued. Would the cook were o' my
mind. Shall we go prove what's to be done?

Borachio

65 We'll wait upon your lordship.   [*Exeunt*

Act 2

Act 2   Scene 1

The family comes together after supper and, all wearing masks, join their guests in a dance. Don Pedro talks of love to Hero; Benedick is abused by Beatrice; Claudio is misled by Don John. The mistake is corrected, Claudio is betrothed to Hero, and Don Pedro forms a plan to trick Beatrice and Benedick into falling in love with each other.

1 *here at supper*: See *1, 3, 62*: Don John must have been too late for the meal.

8 *image*: statue.
9 *my lady's . . . son*: i.e. a spoiled child.

13–14 *money . . . purse*: The words probably carry sexual innuendo ('money' = semen).
15 *a*: he.

17 *shrewd*: sharp, astringent.

18 *curst*: sarcastic.

Scene 1

> *Enter* Leonato, Antonio *his brother,* Hero *his daughter, and* Beatrice *his niece*

Leonato
Was not Count John here at supper?

Antonio
I saw him not.

Beatrice
How tartly that gentleman looks. I never can see him but I am heartburned an hour after.

Hero
5 He is of a very melancholy disposition.

Beatrice
He were an excellent man that were made just in the midway between him and Benedick. The one is too like an image and says nothing, and the other too like my lady's eldest son, evermore tattling.

Leonato
10 Then half Signor Benedick's tongue in Count John's mouth, and half Count John's melancholy in Signor Benedick's face—

Beatrice
With a good leg and a good foot, uncle, and money enough in his purse, such a man would win any
15 woman in the world, if a could get her good will.

Leonato
By my troth, niece, thou wilt never get thee a husband if thou be so shrewd of thy tongue.

Antonio
In faith, she's too curst.

20–1 *God . . . horns*: A proverbial
        expression: the 'curst cow' can do little
        harm with short horns.

23   *no husband*: Talk of 'horns' inevitably
        leads to thoughts of cuckoldry—even
        among ladies.

26–7 *lie . . . woollen*: sleep between blankets
        (without sheets).

35   *in earnest*: as a down payment on a
        contract.
        bearherd: animal showman (who kept
        bears for baiting and other creatures for
        show).
        lead . . . hell: Proverbially said to be the
        fate of unmarried women (although the
        expression has never been satisfactorily
        explained).

41   *Saint Peter*: the keeper of the gates of
        heaven (Matthew 16:19).
        fore the heavens: outside the gate of
        heaven; the Folio's reading ('for the
        heavens') could also be an interjection
        or a mild oath.

42   *bachelors*: The word was then applied to
        both sexes.

Beatrice

Too curst is more than curst. I shall lessen God's
20 sending that way, for it is said God sends a curst cow
short horns, but to a cow too curst he sends none.

Leonato

So, by being too curst, God will send you no horns.

Beatrice

Just, if he send me no husband; for the which
blessing I am at him upon my knees every morning
25 and evening. Lord, I could not endure a husband
with a beard on his face. I had rather lie in the
woollen.

Leonato

You may light on a husband that hath no beard.

Beatrice

What should I do with him? Dress him in my apparel
30 and make him my waiting gentlewoman? He that
hath a beard is more than a youth, and he that hath
no beard is less than a man; and he that is more than
a youth is not for me, and he that is less than a man,
I am not for him. Therefore I will even take sixpence
35 in earnest of the bearherd and lead his apes into hell.

Leonato

Well then, go you into hell?

Beatrice

No, but to the gate, and there will the devil meet me
like an old cuckold with horns on his head, and say,
'Get you to heaven, Beatrice, get you to heaven.
40 Here's no place for you maids.' So deliver I up my
apes, and away to Saint Peter fore the heavens. He
shows me where the bachelors sit, and there live we
as merry as the day is long.

Antonio

[*To* Hero] Well, niece, I trust you will be ruled by
45 your father.

Beatrice

Yes, faith, it is my cousin's duty to make curtsy and
say, 'Father, as it please you.' But yet for all that,
cousin, let him be a handsome fellow, or else make
another curtsy and say, 'Father, as it please me.'

Leonato

50 Well, niece, I hope to see you one day fitted with a
husband.

52 *mettle*: material—with a pun on 'mettle' = spirit.
53 *earth*: 'God formed man of the dust of the ground' (Genesis 2:7).
55 *marl*: clay.
56–7 *Adam's . . . kindred*: Beatrice argues that all men must be descended from Adam (the first man), and therefore related; but the church forbids the marriage of close relatives.

62 *in good time*: at the appropriate moment *and* in the proper rhythm.
    important: importunate, demanding.
63 *measure*: proportion *and* rhythm.

69 *ancientry*: tradition.
70 *bad legs*: perhaps caused by old age.
    cinquepace: Beatrice can pun on the name (pronounced 'sink-apace') of this dance (a sequence of five steps followed by a great leap).
72 *passing*: very.
75s.d. *don masks*: In a pretence of anonymity (which would permit a more free conversation), the Elizabethans wore elaborate, often grotesque, face masks in their festivities.

77 *a bout*: a turn about the dance floor.
78 *friend*: lover.

Beatrice

Not till God make men of some other mettle than earth. Would it not grieve a woman to be overmastered with a piece of valiant dust, to make an
55 account of her life to a clod of wayward marl? No, uncle, I'll none. Adam's sons are my brethren, and truly I hold it a sin to match in my kindred.

Leonato

[*To* Hero] Daughter, remember what I told you. If the prince do solicit you in that kind, you know your
60 answer.

Beatrice

The fault will be in the music, cousin, if you be not wooed in good time. If the prince be too important, tell him there is measure in everything, and so dance out the answer. For hear me, Hero, wooing,
65 wedding, and repenting is as a Scotch jig, a measure, and a cinquepace. The first suit is hot and hasty, like a Scotch jig and full as fantastical; the wedding mannerly modest, as a measure, full of state and ancientry. And then comes repentance, and with his
70 bad legs falls into the cinquepace faster and faster till he sink into his grave.

Leonato

Cousin, you apprehend passing shrewdly.

Beatrice

I have a good eye, uncle; I can see a church by daylight.

Leonato

75 [*To* Antonio] The revellers are entering, brother.

He signals to the others to disperse and don masks

Make good room.

Enter Don Pedro, Claudio, Benedick, Balthasar, [Margaret and Ursula], all masked; Don John and Borachio, [unmasked]; and Attendants and Musicians, among them a drummer

Don Pedro

[*To* Hero] Lady, will you walk a bout with your friend?

Hero

80 So you walk softly, and look sweetly, and say nothing, I am yours for the walk; and especially when I walk away.

Don Pedro

With me in your company?

Hero

I may say so when I please.

Don Pedro

And when please you to say so?

Hero

85 When I like your favour; for God defend the lute should be like the case.

Don Pedro

My visor is Philemon's roof.

Within the house is Jove.

Hero

Why, then, your visor should be thatched.

Don Pedro

90 Speak low if you speak love.

They move aside

Balthasar

[*To* Margaret] Well, I would you did like me.

Margaret

So would not I for your own sake, for I have many ill qualities.

Balthasar

Which is one?

Margaret

95 I say my prayers aloud.

Balthasar

I love you the better; the hearers may cry amen.

Margaret

God match me with a good dancer.

Balthasar

Amen.

Margaret

And God keep him out of my sight when the dance
100 is done. Answer, clerk.

Balthasar

No more words. The clerk is answered.

85 *favour*: face.
   defend: forbid.
86 *case*: Don Pedro was probably wearing a grotesque mask.
87 *Philemon*: A peasant who, with his wife Baucis, entertained the gods unawares in their humble cottage; the story is told in Ovid's *Metamorphoses*, which was translated by Arthur Golding into English rhymed verse with fourteen syllables—imitated here in lines 87–90.
89 *thatched*: i.e. like the roof of Philemon's cottage.

100 *clerk*: The parish clerk made responses to the priest.
101 *answered*: Balthasar has understood Margaret's rejection.

They move aside

Ursula
[*To* Antonio] I know you well enough, you are Signor
Antonio.

Antonio
At a word, I am not.

Ursula
105 I know you by the waggling of your head.

Antonio
To tell you true, I counterfeit him.

Ursula
You could never do him so ill-well unless you were
the very man. Here's his dry hand up and down. You
are he, you are he.

Antonio
110 At a word, I am not.

Ursula
Come, come, do you think I do not know you by your
excellent wit? Can virtue hide itself? Go to, mum,
you are he. Graces will appear, and there's an end.

They move aside

Beatrice
[*To* Benedick] Will you not tell me who told you so?

Benedick
115 No, you shall pardon me.

Beatrice
Nor will you not tell me who you are?

Benedick
Not now.

Beatrice
That I was disdainful, and that I had my good wit
out of the 'Hundred Merry Tales'—well, this was
120 Signor Benedick that said so.

Benedick
What's he?

Beatrice
I am sure you know him well enough.

Benedick
Not I, believe me.

Beatrice
Did he never make you laugh?

108 *dry*: withered.
     up and down: exactly.

112 *mum*: be quiet, no more talk.

119 *Hundred Merry Tales*: a collection of
     comic anecdotes, first published in 1526
     and reprinted many times.

126–7 *Only his gift*: his only talent.

129–30 *pleases . . . them*: amuses some men (by abusing others) and angers those he slanders.
131 *fleet*: company, assembly.
132 *boarded me*: tried it on with me.

135 *break a comparison*: See below, lines 221–42.
136 *peradventure*: perhaps.

143 *amorous on*: in love with.

146 *visor*: mask.

151 *near . . . love*: intimate with my brother.

Benedick

125 I pray you, what is he?

Beatrice

Why, he is the prince's jester, a very dull fool. Only his gift is in devising impossible slanders. None but libertines delight in him, and the commendation is not in his wit but in his villainy, for he both pleases

130 men and angers them, and then they laugh at him and beat him. I am sure he is in the fleet. I would he had boarded me.

Benedick

When I know the gentleman, I'll tell him what you say.

Beatrice

135 Do, do. He'll but break a comparison or two on me, which peradventure not marked, or not laughed at, strikes him into melancholy, and then there's a partridge wing saved, for the fool will eat no supper that night. [*Music*] We must follow the leaders.

Benedick

140 In every good thing.

Beatrice

Nay, if they lead to any ill I will leave them at the next turning.

They dance off.

[*Exeunt all but* Don John, Borachio, *and* Claudio

Don John

[*Aside to* Borachio] Sure my brother is amorous on Hero, and hath withdrawn her father to break with

145 him about it. The ladies follow her, and but one visor remains.

Borachio

[*Aside to* Don John] And that is Claudio. I know him by his bearing.

Don John

[*Approaching* Claudio] Are not you Signor Benedick?

Claudio

150 You know me well. I am he.

Don John

Signor, you are very near my brother in his love. He is enamoured on Hero. I pray you dissuade him from

her. She is no equal for his birth. You may do the
part of an honest man in it.

Claudio

155 How know you he loves her?

Don John

I heard him swear his affection.

Borachio

So did I, too, and he swore he would marry her
tonight.

Don John

Come, let us to the banquet.

[*Exeunt all but* Claudio

Claudio

160 Thus answer I in name of Benedick,
But hear these ill news with the ears of Claudio.
'Tis certain so; the prince woos for himself.
Friendship is constant in all other things
Save in the office and affairs of love.

165 Therefore all hearts in love use their own tongues.
Let every eye negotiate for itself,
And trust no agent; for beauty is a witch
Against whose charms faith melteth into blood.
This is an accident of hourly proof,

170 Which I mistrusted not. Farewell, therefore, Hero.

Enter Benedick

Benedick

Count Claudio?

Claudio

Yea, the same.

Benedick

Come, will you go with me?

Claudio

Whither?

Benedick

175 Even to the next willow, about your own business,
County. What fashion will you wear the garland of?
About your neck, like an usurer's chain? Or under
your arm, like a lieutenant's scarf? You must wear it
one way, for the prince hath got your Hero.

Claudio

180 I wish him joy of her.

159 *banquet*: a dessert course of wine, fruit,
and sweets served after the dancing.
165 *all hearts . . . tongues*: let all lovers speak
for themselves.
168 *faith*: loyalty.
blood: sexual desire.
169 *accident . . . proof*: something that
happens all the time.
170 *mistrusted not*: did not suspect.
175 *willow*: The willow tree was an emblem
of unrequited love.

176 *County*: count; the variant has no
significance.
176–8 *What . . . scarf*: i.e. 'What are you
going to do about it—demand
compensation or challenge the prince to
a duel?'
177 *usurer's chain*: the rich gold chain worn
by a moneylender.
178 *lieutenant's scarf*: military sash worn
diagonally from the shoulder to denote
rank.

181 *drover*: cattle-dealer.

185–6 *strike . . . post*: hit out wildly; the
allusion is to a Spanish story (translated
into English in 1586) about a servant
who deceived his cruel master, a blind
man, into hitting a pillar.
187 *If . . . be*: if you won't leave me.

192 *so*: i.e. I being merry.

194 *puts . . . person*: thinks everybody shares
her opinions.
gives me out: reports me.

197 *Lady Fame*: the personification of
rumour.
198–9 *lodge . . . warren*: game-keeper's hovel
in a park (whose loneliness might
encourage melancholy).

205 *flat*: certain, undeniable.

Benedick
Why, that's spoken like an honest drover; so they sell
bullocks. But did you think the prince would have
served you thus?
Claudio
I pray you leave me.
Benedick
185 Ho, now you strike like the blind man. 'Twas the boy
that stole your meat, and you'll beat the post.
Claudio
If it will not be, I'll leave you.   [*Exit*
Benedick
Alas, poor hurt fowl, now will he creep into
sedges.—But that my Lady Beatrice should know
190 me, and not know me! The prince's fool! Ha, it may
be I go under that title because I am merry. Yea, but
so I am apt to do myself wrong. I am not so reputed!
It is the base and bitter disposition of Beatrice that
puts the world into her person, and so gives me out.
195 Well, I'll be revenged as I may.

Enter Don Pedro

Don Pedro
Now, signor, where's the count? Did you see him?
Benedick
Troth, my lord, I have played the part of Lady Fame.
I found him here as melancholy as a lodge in a
warren. I told him—and I think I told him true—
200 that your grace had got the good will of this young
lady, and I offered him my company to a willow tree,
either to make him a garland, as being forsaken, or
to bind him up a rod, as being worthy to be whipped.
Don Pedro
To be whipped? What's his fault?
Benedick
205 The flat transgression of a schoolboy who, being
overjoyed with finding a bird's nest, shows it his
companion, and he steals it.
Don Pedro
Wilt thou make a trust a transgression? The
transgression is in the stealer.

214 *them*: i.e. the birds.

216 *their singing . . . saying*: they sing what you say you have taught them.

226 *a great thaw*: This might be 'dull' because it kept everyone indoors.

227 *impossible conveyance*: incredible skill.

228 *at a mark*: next to an archery target (signalling the results).

229 *poniards*: daggers.

230 *her terminations*: the pointed endings of her sentences, her terms (of abuse).

233–4 *all . . . transgressed*: i.e. the whole earth (which Adam forfeited when he fell from God's grace—Genesis, chapter 3).

234–6 *She would . . . too*: Hercules, the superman of classical mythology, was forced by Omphale to wear women's clothing and to spin cloth whilst she took away his club and the lion skin which he wore.

235 *turned spit*: turned the handle of the spit (for roasting meat).

237 *Ate . . . apparel*: The goddess of Discord, who (traditionally) was well dressed.

237–8 *some scholar . . . her*: some learned man (knowing Latin) would cast the devil out of her.

Benedick

210 Yet it had not been amiss the rod had been made, and the garland too, for the garland he might have worn himself, and the rod he might have bestowed on you, who, as I take it, have stolen his bird's nest.

Don Pedro

I will but teach them to sing, and restore them to the 215 owner.

Benedick

If their singing answer your saying, by my faith you say honestly.

Don Pedro

The Lady Beatrice hath a quarrel to you. The gentleman that danced with her told her she is much 220 wronged by you.

Benedick

O, she misused me past the endurance of a block. An oak but with one green leaf on it would have answered her. My very visor began to assume life and scold with her. She told me, not thinking I had 225 been myself, that I was the prince's jester, that I was duller than a great thaw, huddling jest upon jest with such impossible conveyance upon me that I stood like a man at a mark, with a whole army shooting at me. She speaks poniards, and every word stabs. If 230 her breath were as terrible as her terminations, there were no living near her; she would infect to the North Star. I would not marry her though she were endowed with all that Adam had left him before he transgressed. She would have made Hercules have 235 turned spit, yea, and have cleft his club to make the fire, too. Come, talk not of her. You shall find her the infernal Ate in good apparel. I would to God some scholar would conjure her, for certainly, while she is here a man may live as quiet in hell as in a sanctuary, 240 and people sin upon purpose because they would go thither. So indeed all disquiet, horror, and perturbation follows her.

244–50 *Will your grace . . . pigmies*: Benedick's list of impossible tasks combines travellers' tales with traditional love trials.

247 *tooth-picker*: Toothpicks, a fashionable Italian innovation, made ideal travel souvenirs.

248 *Prester John*: a legendary king supposed to rule a Christian country in Africa or Asia.

249 *Great Cham*: Kubla Khan, sovereign Prince of Tartary.

250 *pigmies*: legendary dwarfs living in Ethiopia and the Far East (the African peoples had not yet been discovered).

251 *harpy*: The harpies (in classical mythology) were malevolent birds with the faces of women.

258–61 *he lent . . . lost it*: Beatrice hints at an earlier relationship with Benedick.

259 *use for*: interest on.
double: i.e. Beatrice (not being possessive in her love) returned Benedick's heart when she gave him her own.

260 *Marry*: by [the Virgin] Mary; a mild oath.

262 *put him down*: got the better of him (in wit).

264–5 *So . . . fools*: Beatrice understands a literal sense to Don Pedro's words.

Enter Claudio *and* Beatrice

Don Pedro
Look, here she comes.

Benedick
Will your grace command me any service to the
245 world's end? I will go on the slightest errand now to the Antipodes that you can devise to send me on. I will fetch you a tooth-picker now from the furthest inch of Asia, bring you the length of Prester John's foot, fetch you a hair off the Great Cham's beard, do
250 you any embassage to the pigmies, rather than hold three words' conference with this harpy. You have no employment for me?

Don Pedro
None but to desire your good company.

Benedick
O God, sir, here's a dish I love not. I cannot endure
255 my Lady Tongue.   [*Exit*

Don Pedro
Come, lady, come, you have lost the heart of Signor Benedick.

Beatrice
Indeed, my lord, he lent it me a while, and I gave him use for it, a double heart for his single one.
260 Marry, once before he won it of me with false dice. Therefore your grace may well say I have lost it.

Don Pedro
You have put him down, lady, you have put him down.

Beatrice
So I would not he should do me, my lord, lest I
265 should prove the mother of fools. I have brought Count Claudio, whom you sent me to seek.

Don Pedro
Why, how now, Count, wherefore are you sad?

Claudio
Not sad, my lord.

Don Pedro
How then? Sick?

Claudio
270 Neither, my lord.

Beatrice

The count is neither sad, nor sick, nor merry, nor well, but civil count, civil as an orange, and something of that jealous complexion.

Don Pedro

I' faith, lady, I think your blazon to be true, though
275 I'll be sworn, if he be so, his conceit is false. Here, Claudio, I have wooed in thy name, and fair Hero is won. I have broke with her father and his good will obtained.

> Don Pedro *signals*; *enter* Leonato *with* Hero

Name the day of marriage, and God give thee joy.

Leonato

280 Count, take of me my daughter, and with her my fortunes. His grace hath made the match, and all grace say amen to it.

Beatrice

Speak, Count, 'tis your cue.

Claudio

Silence is the perfectest herald of joy. I were but little
285 happy if I could say how much. [*To* Hero] Lady, as you are mine, I am yours. I give away myself for you, and dote upon the exchange.

Beatrice

[*To* Hero] Speak, cousin; or, if you cannot, stop his mouth with a kiss, and let not him speak, neither.

Don Pedro

290 In faith, lady, you have a merry heart.

Beatrice

Yea, my lord. I thank it, poor fool, it keeps on the windy side of care.—My cousin tells him in his ear that he is in her heart.

Claudio

And so she doth, cousin.

Beatrice

295 Good Lord, for alliance! Thus goes everyone to the world but I, and I am sunburnt. I may sit in a corner and cry 'Heigh-ho for a husband.'

Don Pedro

Lady Beatrice, I will get you one.

272 *civil*: A pun with 'Seville' leads to the thought of bitter oranges and the colour—yellow—of jealousy.

274 *blazon*: heraldic description.

275 *conceit*: notion, understanding.

277 *broke with*: spoken to.

280–2 *Count . . . to it*: Leonato's formal language makes this engagement official and binding—a 'marriage by pre-contract'.

291 *poor fool*: poor old thing.

292 *windy . . . care*: upwind of trouble.

295 *Good . . . alliance*: Beatrice reacts to Claudio's 'cousin' (line 294).

295–6 *Thus . . . world*: that's the way of the world for everyone.

296 *sunburnt*: A suntan was unfashionable and undesirable in Elizabethan England.

297 *cry . . . husband*: go whistle for a husband.

299 *getting*: begetting.

310 *cried*: in labour.

317 *melancholy element*: i.e. black bile;
human beings were thought to be made
up of four elements (blood, phlegm,
and choler were the others), and the
dominance of any one of these
determined the individual
temperament.
318 *sad*: serious.
319 *ever*: always.
323–4 *out of suit*: out of courtship.

Beatrice

I would rather have one of your father's getting. Hath
300 your grace ne'er a brother like you? Your father got
excellent husbands if a maid could come by them.

Don Pedro

Will you have me, lady?

Beatrice

No, my lord, unless I might have another for
working days. Your grace is too costly to wear every
305 day. But I beseech your grace, pardon me; I was
born to speak all mirth and no matter.

Don Pedro

Your silence most offends me, and to be merry best
becomes you; for out o' question, you were born in
a merry hour.

Beatrice

310 No, sure, my lord, my mother cried. But then there
was a star danced, and under that was I born. [*To
Hero and* Claudio] Cousins, God give you joy.

Leonato

Niece, will you look to those things I told you of?

Beatrice

I cry you mercy, uncle. [*To* Don Pedro] By your
315 grace's pardon.   [*Exit* Beatrice

Don Pedro

By my troth, a pleasant-spirited lady.

Leonato

There's little of the melancholy element in her, my
lord. She is never sad but when she sleeps, and not
ever sad then; for I have heard my daughter say she
320 hath often dreamt of unhappiness and waked herself
with laughing.

Don Pedro

She cannot endure to hear tell of a husband.

Leonato

O, by no means. She mocks all her wooers out of
suit.

Don Pedro

325 She were an excellent wife for Benedick.

Leonato

O Lord! My lord, if they were but a week married
they would talk themselves mad.

Don Pedro
County Claudio, when mean you to go to church?
Claudio
Tomorrow, my lord. Time goes on crutches till love
330 have all his rites.
Leonato
Not till Monday, my dear son, which is hence a just
sevennight; and a time too brief, too, to have all
things answer my mind.
Don Pedro
Come, you shake the head at so long a breathing, but
335 I warrant thee, Claudio, the time shall not go dully
by us. I will in the interim undertake one of
Hercules' labours, which is to bring Signor Benedick
and the Lady Beatrice into a mountain of affection
th'one with th'other. I would fain have it a match,
340 and I doubt not but to fashion it, if you three will but
minister such assistance as I shall give you direction.
Leonato
My lord, I am for you, though it cost me ten nights'
watchings.
Claudio
And I, my lord.
Don Pedro
345 And you too, gentle Hero?
Hero
I will do any modest office, my lord, to help my
cousin to a good husband.
Don Pedro
And Benedick is not the unhopefullest husband that
I know. Thus far can I praise him: he is of a noble
350 strain, of approved valour and confirmed honesty. I
will teach you how to humour your cousin that she
shall fall in love with Benedick; and I, with your two
helps, will so practise on Benedick that, in despite of
his quick wit and his queasy stomach, he shall fall in
355 love with Beatrice. If we can do this, Cupid is no
longer an archer; his glory shall be ours, for we are
the only love-gods. Go in with me, and I will tell you
my drift.   [*Exeunt*

331–2 *a just sevennight*: exactly a week.

333 *answer my mind*: just as I want them.

334 *breathing*: pause, delay.

336 *interim*: meantime.
337 *Hercules' labours*: The demi-god of classical mythology demonstrated his divine nature by accomplishing twelve near-impossible tasks.
339 *would fain*: would like to.

342–3 *nights' watchings*: sleepless nights.

350 *strain*: lineage.
approved: tested (in battle).

353 *practise on*: influence, work upon.
354 *queasy stomach*: This would give him little appetite (for marriage).

358 *drift*: intentions.

Don John is delighted when Borachio
proposes a scheme to discredit Hero.

3 *cross*: obstruct, thwart.

6–7 *whatsoever . . . mine*: whatever goes
    against his wishes goes along with mine.

20 *temper*: concoct.

23 *estimation*: merit, quality.

24 *stale*: whore.

26 *misuse*: abuse.
    vex: torment.

Scene 2

Enter Don John *and* Borachio

Don John
It is so. The Count Claudio shall marry the daughter
of Leonato.

Borachio
Yea, my lord, but I can cross it.

Don John
Any bar, any cross, any impediment will be
5 medicinable to me. I am sick in displeasure to him,
and whatsoever comes athwart his affection ranges
evenly with mine. How canst thou cross this
marriage?

Borachio
Not honestly, my lord, but so covertly that no
10 dishonesty shall appear in me.

Don John
Show me briefly how.

Borachio
I think I told your lordship a year since how much I
am in the favour of Margaret, the waiting
gentlewoman to Hero.

Don John
15 I remember.

Borachio
I can at any unseasonable instant of the night
appoint her to look out at her lady's chamber
window.

Don John
What life is in that to be the death of this marriage?

Borachio
20 The poison of that lies in you to temper. Go you to
the prince your brother. Spare not to tell him that he
hath wronged his honour in marrying the renowned
Claudio—whose estimation do you mightily hold
up—to a contaminated stale, such a one as Hero.

Don John
25 What proof shall I make of that?

Borachio
Proof enough to misuse the prince, to vex Claudio,
to undo Hero and kill Leonato. Look you for any
other issue?

29 *Only*: for no other reason but.

30 *meet*: fitting.

32 *Intend*: pretend.

35 *cozened*: deceived, cheated.
36 *semblance of a maid*: i.e. a virgin in
      appearance only.
37 *discovered*: revealed.
38–9 *Offer . . . likelihood*: give them
      examples which will be no more
      unlikely.

45 *jealousy*: suspicion.
46 *assurance*: proof.

48 *cunning*: clever.

Don John
Only to despite them I will endeavour anything.
Borachio
30 Go then. Find me a meet hour to draw Don Pedro
and the Count Claudio alone. Tell them that you
know that Hero loves me. Intend a kind of zeal both
to the prince and Claudio—as in love of your
brother's honour who hath made this match, and his
35 friend's reputation who is thus like to be cozened
with the semblance of a maid—that you have
discovered thus. They will scarcely believe this
without trial. Offer them instances, which shall bear
no less likelihood than to see me at her chamber
40 window, hear me call Margaret Hero, hear Margaret
term me Claudio. And bring them to see this the
very night before the intended wedding, for in the
meantime I will so fashion the matter that Hero shall
be absent, and there shall appear such seeming truth
45 of Hero's disloyalty that jealousy shall be called
assurance, and all the preparation overthrown.
Don John
Grow this to what adverse issue it can, I will put it in
practice. Be cunning in the working of this, and thy
fee is a thousand ducats.
Borachio
50 Be you constant in the accusation, and my cunning
shall not shame me.
Don John
I will presently go learn their day of marriage.
                                              [*Exeunt*

Act 2   Scene 3

Benedick is tricked into believing that
Beatrice is in love with him.

5 *I . . . already*: I'll be back immediately:
but Benedick deliberately
misunderstands.

11 *argument*: subject.

13 *drum . . . fife*: i.e. military music.

14 *tabor*: small drum usually played on
festival occasions.

17 *carving*: designing.
doublet: garment, with detachable
sleeves, for man's upper body.

20 *orthography*: rhetorician.

22 *converted*: transformed.

25 *oyster*: i.e. the lowest form of animal life
(in the Elizabethan hierarchy).

31 *cheapen*: make a bid for.

32 *Noble*: Benedick couples the usual sense
with the name of a coin (33p in today's
money).

33 *angel*: coin worth 50p.

Scene 3

Enter Benedick

Benedick

Boy!

Enter Boy

Boy

Signor?

Benedick

In my chamber window lies a book. Bring it hither to
me in the orchard.

Boy

5 I am here already, sir.

Benedick

I know that, but I would have thee hence and here
again. [*Exit* Boy] I do much wonder that one man,
seeing how much another man is a fool when he
dedicates his behaviours to love, will, after he hath

10 laughed at such shallow follies in others, become the
argument of his own scorn by falling in love. And
such a man is Claudio. I have known when there was
no music with him but the drum and the fife, and
now had he rather hear the tabor and the pipe. I have

15 known when he would have walked ten mile afoot to
see a good armour, and now will he lie ten nights
awake carving the fashion of a new doublet. He was
wont to speak plain and to the purpose, like an
honest man and a soldier, and now is he turned

20 orthography. His words are a very fantastical
banquet, just so many strange dishes. May I be so
converted and see with these eyes? I cannot tell; I
think not. I will not be sworn but love may transform
me to an oyster. But I'll take my oath on it: till he

25 have made an oyster of me he shall never make me
such a fool. One woman is fair, yet I am well.
Another is wise, yet I am well. Another virtuous, yet
I am well. But till all graces be in one woman, one
woman shall not come in my grace. Rich she shall

30 be, that's certain. Wise, or I'll none. Virtuous, or I'll
never cheapen her. Fair, or I'll never look on her.
Mild, or come not near me. Noble, or not I for an
angel. Of good discourse, an excellent musician, and

her hair shall be of what colour it please God.—Ha!
35 The prince and Monsieur Love. I will hide me in the
arbour.

He hides. Enter Don Pedro, Leonato, *and*
Claudio

Don Pedro
Come, shall we hear this music?
   Claudio
Yea, my good lord. How still the evening is,
As hush'd on purpose to grace harmony.
   Don Pedro
40 [*Aside*] See you where Benedick hath hid himself?
   Claudio
[*Aside*] O, very well, my lord. The music ended,
We'll fit the hid fox with a pennyworth.

Enter Balthasar *with music*

Don Pedro
Come, Balthasar, we'll hear that song again.
   Balthasar
O good my lord, tax not so bad a voice
45 To slander music any more than once.
   Don Pedro
It is the witness still of excellency
To put a strange face on his own perfection.
I pray thee sing, and let me woo no more.
   Balthasar
Because you talk of wooing I will sing,
50 Since many a wooer doth commence his suit
To her he thinks not worthy, yet he woos.
Yet will he swear he loves.
   Don Pedro
                                   Nay, pray thee, come;
Or if thou wilt hold longer argument,
Do it in notes.
   Balthasar
                      Note this before my notes:
55 There's not a note of mine that's worth the noting.
   Don Pedro
Why, these are very crotchets that he speaks.
Note notes, forsooth, and nothing!

42 *pennyworth*: value for his money.

44 *tax*: make demands on.

46 *witness*: proof, evidence.
   still: always.
47 *put . . . on*: pretend not to recognize.

56 *crotchets*: quarter notes *and*
   eccentricities.
57 *nothing*: nothing else; Don Pedro is tired
   of Balthasar's quibbling.

The accompaniment begins

Benedick

Now, divine air! Now is his soul ravished. Is it not
strange that sheep's guts should hale souls out of
60 men's bodies? Well, a horn for my money, when all's
done.

Balthasar

[*Sings*]

Sigh no more, ladies, sigh no more.
    Men were deceivers ever,
One foot in sea, and one on shore,
65   To one thing constant never.
Then sigh not so, but let them go,
    And be you blithe and bonny,
Converting all your sounds of woe
    Into hey nonny, nonny.

70   Sing no more ditties, sing no more
        Of dumps so dull and heavy.
    The fraud of men was ever so
        Since summer first was leafy.
    Then sigh not so, but let them go,
75   And be you blithe and bonny,
    Converting all your sounds of woe
        Into hey nonny, nonny.

Don Pedro

By my troth, a good song.

Balthasar

And an ill singer, my lord.

Don Pedro

80 Ha, no, no, faith. Thou sing'st well enough for a
shift.

Benedick

[*Aside*] An he had been a dog that should have
howled thus, they would have hanged him. And I
pray God his bad voice bode no mischief. I had as
85 lief have heard the night-raven, come what plague
could have come after it.

Don Pedro

Yea, marry, dost thou hear, Balthasar? I pray thee get
us some excellent music, for tomorrow night we
would have it at the Lady Hero's chamber window.

59 *sheep's guts*: i.e. a stringed instrument
(probably a lute).
hale: draw.
60 *horn*: hunting horn.

71 *dumps*: mournful melodies.

81–1 *for a shift*: as a makeshift.

82 *An*: if.

84–5 *as lief*: rather.
85 *night-raven*: a bird of ill omen.

88 *some excellent music*: This music is never
mentioned again.

Balthasar

90 The best I can, my lord.

Don Pedro

Do so. Farewell.   [*Exit* Balthasar

Come hither, Leonato. What was it you told me of
today, that your niece Beatrice was in love with
Signor Benedick?

Claudio

95 [*Aside*] O, ay, stalk on, stalk on; the fowl sits. [*Raising
his voice*] I did never think that lady would have loved
any man.

Leonato

No, nor I neither. But most wonderful that she
should so dote on Signor Benedick, whom she hath

100 in all outward behaviours seemed ever to abhor.

Benedick

[*Aside*] Is't possible? Sits the wind in that corner?

Leonato

By my troth, my lord, I cannot tell what to think of
it. But that she loves him with an enraged affection,
it is past the infinite of thought.

Don Pedro

105 Maybe she doth but counterfeit.

Claudio

Faith, like enough.

Leonato

O God! Counterfeit? There was never counterfeit of
passion came so near the life of passion as she
discovers it.

Don Pedro

110 Why, what effects of passion shows she?

Claudio

[*Aside*] Bait the hook well. This fish will bite.

Leonato

What effects, my lord? She will sit you—you heard
my daughter tell you how.

Claudio

She did indeed.

Don Pedro

115 How, how, I pray you? You amaze me. I would have
thought her spirit had been invincible against all
assaults of affection.

95 *stalk on*: i.e. proceed like hunters hiding
behind a stalking horse.
the fowl sits: he's a sitting duck.

101 *Sits . . . corner*: is that how things are.

104 *it is . . . thought*: i.e. no amount of
thinking can understand.

109 *discovers*: shows.

112 *sit you*: The 'ethical dative', used here in
an attempt to arouse interest when
words fail.

Leonato

I would have sworn it had, my lord, especially against Benedick.

Benedick

120 [*Aside*] I should think this a gull, but that the white-bearded fellow speaks it. Knavery cannot, sure, hide himself in such reverence.

Claudio

[*Aside*] He hath ta'en th'infection. Hold it up.

Don Pedro

Hath she made her affection known to Benedick?

Leonato

125 No, and swears she never will. That's her torment.

Claudio

'Tis true, indeed, so your daughter says. 'Shall I,' says she, 'that have so oft encountered him with scorn, write to him that I love him?'

Leonato

This says she now when she is beginning to write to
130 him; for she'll be up twenty times a night, and there will she sit in her smock till she have writ a sheet of paper. My daughter tells us all.

Claudio

Now you talk of a sheet of paper, I remember a pretty jest your daughter told us of.

Leonato

135 O, when she had writ it and was reading it over, she found 'Benedick' and 'Beatrice' between the sheet.

Claudio

That.

Leonato

O, she tore the letter into a thousand halfpence, railed at herself that she should be so immodest to
140 write to one that she knew would flout her. 'I measure him,' says she, 'by my own spirit, for I should flout him if he writ to me. Yea, though I loved him I should.'

Claudio

Then down upon her knees she falls, weeps, sobs,
145 beats her heart, tears her hair, prays, curses. 'O sweet Benedick! God give me patience.'

---

120 *gull*: trick.

131 *smock*: slip, under-garment.

136 *between the sheet*: i.e. the bedsheets.

137 *That*: Claudio expresses disappointment that Leonato tells such an old joke so badly.
138 *halfpence*: little coins.

148   *ecstasy*: frenzy.

155   *an alms*: an act of charity.

160   *blood*: passion.

165   *doffed*: put aside.

167   *a*: he.

172   *bate*: abate.

174   *make tender of*: offer.

176   *contemptible*: contemptuous.

177   *proper*: attractive, good-looking.

Leonato

She doth indeed; my daughter says so. And the ecstasy hath so much overborne her that my daughter is sometime afeard she will do a desperate
150 outrage to herself. It is very true.

Don Pedro

It were good that Benedick knew of it by some other, if she will not discover it.

Claudio

To what end? He would make but a sport of it and torment the poor lady worse.

Don Pedro

155 An he should, it were an alms to hang him. She's an excellent sweet lady and, out of all suspicion, she is virtuous.

Claudio

And she is exceeding wise.

Don Pedro

In everything but in loving Benedick.

Leonato

160 O my lord, wisdom and blood combating in so tender a body, we have ten proofs to one that blood hath the victory. I am sorry for her, as I have just cause, being her uncle and her guardian.

Don Pedro

I would she had bestowed this dotage on me. I
165 would have doffed all other respects and made her half myself. I pray you tell Benedick of it, and hear what a will say.

Leonato

Were it good, think you?

Claudio

Hero thinks surely she will die; for she says she will
170 die if he love her not, and she will die ere she make her love known, and she will die if he woo her, rather than she will bate one breath of her accustomed crossness.

Don Pedro

She doth well. If she should make tender of her love
175 'tis very possible he'll scorn it, for the man, as you know all, hath a contemptible spirit.

Claudio

He is a very proper man.

178 *outward happiness*: appearance.

180 *wit*: intelligence.

182 *Hector*: the Trojan champion.

190 *large*: broad, improper.

193 *wear it out*: get over it, learn to accept things.

202 *upon*: after.

207 *no such matter*: there will be nothing in it.

Don Pedro
He hath indeed a good outward happiness.
Claudio
Before God, and in my mind, very wise.
Don Pedro
180 He doth indeed show some sparks that are like wit.
Claudio
And I take him to be valiant.
Don Pedro
As Hector, I assure you. And in the managing of quarrels you may say he is wise, for either he avoids them with great discretion or undertakes them with
185 a most Christianlike fear.
Leonato
If he do fear God, a must necessarily keep peace. If he break the peace, he ought to enter into a quarrel with fear and trembling.
Don Pedro
And so will he do, for the man doth fear God,
190 howsoever it seems not in him by some large jests he will make. Well, I am sorry for your niece. Shall we go seek Benedick and tell him of her love?
Claudio
Never tell him, my lord. Let her wear it out with good counsel.
Leonato
195 Nay, that's impossible. She may wear her heart out first.
Don Pedro
Well, we will hear further of it by your daughter. Let it cool the while. I love Benedick well, and I could wish he would modestly examine himself to see how
200 much he is unworthy so good a lady.
Leonato
My lord, will you walk? Dinner is ready.
Claudio
[*Aside*] If he do not dote on her upon this, I will never trust my expectation.
Don Pedro
[*Aside*] Let there be the same net spread for her,
205 and that must your daughter and her gentlewomen carry. The sport will be when they hold one opinion of the other's dotage, and no such matter. That's the

208–9 *dumb show*: mime (because they will be speechless with embarrassment).

211 *sadly*: seriously.

213 *have . . . bent*: are fully stretched (like a bow).

221 *reprove*: disprove, doubt.

223 *argument*: evidence.
224 *horribly*: exceedingly.

228 *meat*: food.
229 *sentences*: maxims, wise sayings.
230–1 *career of his humour*: pursuit of his inclination.

238 *Fair Beatrice . . . pains*: Benedick thanks Beatrice with a regular blank verse line.

scene that I would see, which will be merely a dumb show. Let us send her to call him in to dinner.

[*Exeunt* Don Pedro, Claudio, *and* Leonato

Benedick

210 [*Coming forward*] This can be no trick. The conference was sadly borne. They have the truth of this from Hero. They seem to pity the lady; it seems her affections have their full bent. Love me? Why, it must be requited. I hear how I am censured. They

215 say I will bear myself proudly if I perceive the love come from her. They say too that she will rather die than give any sign of affection. I did never think to marry. I must not seem proud. Happy are they that hear their detractions and can put them to mending.

220 They say the lady is fair; 'tis a truth, I can bear them witness. And virtuous; 'tis so, I cannot reprove it. And wise, but for loving me. By my troth, it is no addition to her wit nor no great argument of her folly, for I will be horribly in love with her. I may

225 chance have some odd quirks and remnants of wit broken on me because I have railed so long against marriage, but doth not the appetite alter? A man loves the meat in his youth that he cannot endure in his age. Shall quips and sentences and these paper

230 bullets of the brain awe a man from the career of his humour? No. The world must be peopled. When I said I would die a bachelor, I did not think I should live till I were married. Here comes Beatrice.

Enter Beatrice

By this day, she's a fair lady. I do spy some marks of

235 love in her.

Beatrice

Against my will I am sent to bid you come in to dinner.

Benedick

Fair Beatrice, I thank you for your pains.

Beatrice

I took no more pains for those thanks than you take

240 pains to thank me. If it had been painful I would not have come.

Benedick

You take pleasure, then, in the message?

244 *daw*: jackdaw.
244–5 *no stomach*: no appetite.

Beatrice

Yea, just so much as you may take upon a knife's point and not choke a daw withal.—You have no
245 stomach, signor? Fare you well.   [*Exit*

Benedick

Ha! 'Against my will I am sent to bid you come in to dinner.' There's a double meaning in that. 'I took no more pains for those thanks than you took pains to thank me.' That's as much as to say 'Any pains that
250 I take for you is as easy as thanks.' If I do not take pity of her I am a villain. If I do not love her I am a Jew. I will go get her picture.   [*Exit*

252 *a Jew*: i.e. have no faith.
   get her picture: Benedick intends to commission a miniature portrait which he can wear, perhaps, as a locket.

Act 3

Act 3 Scene 1

Beatrice is tricked into believing that Benedick is in love with her.

1 *parlour*: a room reserved for private family use.

3 *Proposing*: conversing.

4 *Ursula*: The Quarto's spelling 'Ursley' probably reflects contemporary pronunciation.

7 *pleached*: pleachèd. See *1*, *2*, *8*.

8–11 *Where . . . bred it*: Hero repeats one of the moral commonplaces of her education.

12 *propose*: conversation.

14 *presently*: immediately.

16 *trace*: pace.

23 *only wounds*: wounds only.

Scene 1

Enter Hero *and two gentlewomen,* Margaret *and* Ursula

Hero
Good Margaret, run thee to the parlour.
There shalt thou find my cousin Beatrice
Proposing with the prince and Claudio.
Whisper her ear, and tell her I and Ursula
5 Walk in the orchard, and our whole discourse
Is all of her. Say that thou overheard'st us,
And bid her steal into the pleached bower
Where honeysuckles, ripened by the sun,
Forbid the sun to enter, like favourites
10 Made proud by princes, that advance their pride
Against that power that bred it. There will she hide
      her
To listen our propose. This is thy office.
Bear thee well in it, and leave us alone.
Margaret
I'll make her come, I warrant you, presently.   [*Exit*
Hero
15 Now, Ursula, when Beatrice doth come,
As we do trace this alley up and down
Our talk must only be of Benedick.
When I do name him, let it be thy part
To praise him more than ever man did merit.
20 My talk to thee must be how Benedick
Is sick in love with Beatrice. Of this matter
Is little Cupid's crafty arrow made,
That only wounds by hearsay.

Enter Beatrice, *who hides*

> Now begin,
> For look where Beatrice like a lapwing runs
> 25 Close by the ground to hear our conference.

Ursula

> [*Aside to* Hero] The pleasant'st angling is to see the fish
> Cut with her golden oars the silver stream
> And greedily devour the treacherous bait.
> So angle we for Beatrice, who even now
> 30 Is couched in the woodbine coverture.
> Fear you not my part of the dialogue.

Hero

> [*Aside to* Ursula] Then go we near her, that her ear lose nothing
> Of the false-sweet bait that we lay for it.

Approaching Beatrice's *hiding-place*

> No, truly, Ursula, she is too disdainful.
> 35 I know her spirits are as coy and wild
> As haggards of the rock.

Ursula

> But are you sure
> That Benedick loves Beatrice so entirely?

Hero

> So says the prince and my new-trothed lord.

Ursula

> And did they bid you tell her of it, madam?

Hero

> 40 They did entreat me to acquaint her of it,
> But I persuaded them, if they lov'd Benedick,
> To wish him wrestle with affection
> And never to let Beatrice know of it.

Ursula

> Why did you so? Doth not the gentleman
> 45 Deserve as full as fortunate a bed
> As ever Beatrice shall couch upon?

Hero

> O god of love! I know he doth deserve
> As much as may be yielded to a man,
> But nature never fram'd a woman's heart
> 50 Of prouder stuff than that of Beatrice.

24 *lapwing*: The lapwing (plover) runs along the ground to draw predators away from its nest.

25 *conference*: conversation.

30 *couched*: couchèd.
woodbine: honeysuckle.
coverture: shelter.

35 *coy*: defiant.
36 *haggards*: wild hawks.

38 *new-trothed*: trothèd; recently betrothed.

45 *as full . . . bed*: just as good a marriage.

52 *Misprising*: undervaluing.
54 *All matter . . . weak*: all other discourse
    seems of little worth.
55 *shape*: image.
   project: idea.
56 *self-endear'd*: in love with herself.
60 *How*: however.
   rarely: handsomely.
61 *spell him backward*: take everything the
   wrong way: Hero proceeds to
   demonstrate her meaning.
63 *black*: dark, swarthy.
   antic: grotesque.
64 *ill-headed*: with a poor head.
65 *agate . . . cut*: Agate stones, often carved
   with human figures, were used on seal-
   rings.

66 *vane*: weather-vane.
67 *moved*: movèd.
70 *simpleness*: integrity.
   purchaseth: earns.
71, 73 *commendable*: The stress is on the
   first syllable.
72 *from*: contrary to.
76 *press . . . wit*: heap jokes upon me until I
   died with laughing; pressing to death,
   '*peine forte et dure*', was the punishment
   inflicted on criminals who refused to
   speak when arraigned before a court.
80 *tickling*: This word needs to be
   pronounced with an extra syllable
   ('tick-el-ing') if the rhythm is to be
   completely regular; see 5, 4, 34.

84 *honest slanders*: harmless lies.

Disdain and scorn ride sparkling in her eyes,
Misprising what they look on, and her wit
Values itself so highly that to her
All matter else seems weak. She cannot love,
55 Nor take no shape nor project of affection,
She is so self-endear'd.
      Ursula
                    Sure, I think so,
And therefore certainly it were not good
She knew his love, lest she'll make sport at it.
      Hero
Why, you speak truth. I never yet saw man,
60 How wise, how noble, young, how rarely featur'd,
But she would spell him backward. If fair-fac'd,
She would swear the gentleman should be her sister;
If black, why nature, drawing of an antic,
Made a foul blot; if tall, a lance ill-headed;
65 If low, an agate very vilely cut;
If speaking, why, a vane blown with all winds;
If silent, why, a block moved with none.
So turns she every man the wrong side out,
And never gives to truth and virtue that
70 Which simpleness and merit purchaseth.
      Ursula
Sure, sure, such carping is not commendable.
      Hero
No, not to be so odd and from all fashions
As Beatrice is cannot be commendable.
But who dare tell her so? If I should speak,
75 She would mock me into air; O, she would laugh me
Out of myself, press me to death with wit.
Therefore let Benedick, like cover'd fire,
Consume away in sighs, waste inwardly.
It were a better death than die with mocks,
80 Which is as bad as die with tickling.
      Ursula
Yet tell her of it; hear what she will say.
      Hero
No. Rather I will go to Benedick
And counsel him to fight against his passion.
And truly, I'll devise some honest slanders
85 To stain my cousin with. One doth not know

How much an ill word may empoison liking.

Ursula

O, do not do your cousin such a wrong.
She cannot be so much without true judgement,
Having so swift and excellent a wit
90 As she is priz'd to have, as to refuse
So rare a gentleman as Signor Benedick.

Hero

He is the only man of Italy,
Always excepted my dear Claudio.

Ursula

I pray you be not angry with me, madam;
95 Speaking my fancy, Signor Benedick,
For shape, for bearing, argument, and valour
Goes foremost in report through Italy.

Hero

Indeed, he hath an excellent good name.

Ursula

His excellence did earn it ere he had it.
100 When are you married, madam?

Hero

Why, every day, tomorrow. Come, go in.
I'll show thee some attires and have thy counsel
Which is the best to furnish me tomorrow.

Ursula

[*Aside*] She's lim'd, I warrant you, we have caught
her, madam.

Hero

105 [*Aside*] If it prove so, then loving goes by haps.
Some Cupid kills with arrows, some with traps.
[*Exeunt* Hero *and* Ursula

Beatrice

[*Coming forward*] What fire is in mine ears? Can this
be true?
Stand I condemn'd for pride and scorn so much?
Contempt, farewell; and maiden pride, adieu.
110 No glory lives behind the back of such.
And, Benedick, love on. I will requite thee,
Taming my wild heart to thy loving hand.
If thou dost love, my kindness shall incite thee
To bind our loves up in a holy band.
115 For others say thou dost deserve, and I
Believe it better than reportingly.   [*Exit*

90 *priz'd*: esteemed.
96 *argument*: discourse.
100 *married*: to be married.
101 *every day, tomorrow*: 'for every day of
my life—but the ceremony is
tomorrow'.
102 *attires*: head-dresses.
104 *lim'd*: caught with bird-lime (a sticky
substance smeared on branches where
the birds were likely to land).

105 *haps*: chances.
107–16 *What . . . reportingly*: Beatrice, like
Benedick at 2, 3, 238, speaks her love in
verse (two rhyming quatrains and a
closing couplet—almost a sonnet).
107 *What . . . ears*: A burning sensation in
the ears is (proverbially) a sign that
someone is talking about you.
112 *Taming . . . heart*: Beatrice remembers
the hawk image of lines 35–6.
114 *band*: bond.
116 *reportingly*: mere hearsay.

Don Pedro and Claudio tease Benedick
about his changed appearance, but their
laughter is silenced by Don John's
insinuations.

3 *bring*: escort.
  vouchsafe: permit.

9–10 *little hangman*: little scamp.

16 *truant*: rogue.

22 *hang . . . draw it*: Hanging and drawing
   (disembowelling) were punishments for
   felons.

24 *humour . . . worm*: It was believed that
   toothache was caused by worms
   breeding in the rotten moisture of a
   hollow tooth.

Scene 2

Enter Don Pedro, Claudio, Benedick, *and*
Leonato

Don Pedro
I do but stay till your marriage be consummate, and
then go I toward Aragon.

Claudio
I'll bring you thither, my lord, if you'll vouchsafe me.

Don Pedro
5 Nay, that would be as great a soil in the new gloss of
your marriage as to show a child his new coat and
forbid him to wear it. I will only be bold with
Benedick for his company, for from the crown of his
head to the sole of his foot he is all mirth. He hath
10 twice or thrice cut Cupid's bowstring, and the little
hangman dare not shoot at him. He hath a heart as
sound as a bell, and his tongue is the clapper, for
what his heart thinks his tongue speaks.

Benedick
Gallants, I am not as I have been.

Leonato
So say I. Methinks you are sadder.

Claudio
15 I hope he be in love.

Don Pedro
Hang him, truant! There's no true drop of blood in
him to be truly touched with love. If he be sad, he
wants money.

Benedick
I have the toothache.

Don Pedro
20 Draw it.

Benedick
Hang it.

Claudio
You must hang it first and draw it afterwards.

Don Pedro
What? Sigh for the toothache?

Leonato
Where is but a humour or a worm.

28 *fancy*: i.e. affection.
   strange disguises: Don Pedro mocks the
   contemporary English trend for
   imitating European fashions.

31 *slops*: voluminous breeches.
40 *old . . . cheek*: Someone must have told
   Benedick how Beatrice said she 'could
   not endure a husband with a beard on
   his face' (2, 1, 25–6).
41 *stuffed tennis balls*: Tennis was played
   with leather balls stuffed with horse-
   hair.
44 *civet*: perfume based on musk taken
   from glands of the civet cat.
47 *note*: indication.
   melancholy: The lover's melancholy was
   a recognized psychological condition.
48 *wash his face*: i.e. with perfume—after-
   shave lotion.
49 *paint himself*: use cosmetics.
51–2 *his . . . stops*: i.e. he has stopped
   joking now and started singing love-
   songs.
52 *by stops*: with frets (like a lute-string).

Benedick

25 Well, everyone can master a grief but he that has it.

Claudio

Yet say I he is in love.

Don Pedro

There is no appearance of fancy in him, unless it be
a fancy that he hath to strange disguises: as to be a
Dutchman today, a Frenchman tomorrow, or in the
30 shape of two countries at once, as a German from
the waist downward, all slops, and a Spaniard from
the hip upward, no doublet. Unless he have a fancy
to this foolery, as it appears he hath, he is no fool for
fancy, as you would have it appear he is.

Claudio

35 If he be not in love with some woman, there is no
believing old signs. A brushes his hat o' mornings;
what should that bode?

Don Pedro

Hath any man seen him at the barber's?

Claudio

No, but the barber's man hath been seen with him,
40 and the old ornament of his cheek hath already
stuffed tennis balls.

Leonato

Indeed, he looks younger than he did by the loss of
a beard.

Don Pedro

Nay, a rubs himself with civet. Can you smell him
45 out by that?

Claudio

That's as much as to say the sweet youth's in love.

Don Pedro

The greatest note of it is his melancholy.

Claudio

And when was he wont to wash his face?

Don Pedro

Yea, or to paint himself? For the which I hear what
50 they say of him.

Claudio

Nay, but his jesting spirit, which is now crept into a
lute-string, and now governed by stops.

Don Pedro
Indeed, that tells a heavy tale for him. Conclude, conclude, he is in love.

Claudio
55 Nay, but I know who loves him.

Don Pedro
That would I know, too. I warrant, one that knows him not.

Claudio
Yes, and his ill conditions, and in despite of all, dies for him.

Don Pedro
60 She shall be buried with her face upwards.

Benedick
Yet is this no charm for the toothache. Old signor, walk aside with me. I have studied eight or nine wise words to speak to you which these hobby-horses must not hear.   [*Exeunt* Benedick *and* Leonato

Don Pedro
65 For my life, to break with him about Beatrice.

Claudio
'Tis even so. Hero and Margaret have by this played their parts with Beatrice, and then the two bears will not bite one another when they meet.

Enter Don John *the Bastard*

Don John
My lord, and brother, God save you.

Don Pedro
70 Good-e'en, brother.

Don John
If your leisure served I would speak with you.

Don Pedro
In private?

Don John
If it please you. Yet Count Claudio may hear, for what I would speak of concerns him.

Don Pedro
75 What's the matter?

Don John
[*To* Claudio] Means your lordship to be married tomorrow?

58 *ill conditions*: bad qualities.
 dies: i.e. in orgasm; Don Pedro's comment in the next line shows that he has understood the sexual innuendo.
60 *buried . . . upwards*: i.e. smothered by Benedick.

63 *hobby-horses*: buffoons (so-called after the stylized horse fastened round the waist of a morris-dancer).

Don Pedro
You know he does.

Don John
I know not that when he knows what I know.

Claudio
80 If there be any impediment, I pray you discover it.

Don John
You may think I love you not. Let that appear
hereafter, and aim better at me by that I now will
manifest. For my brother, I think he holds you well,
and in dearness of heart hath holp to effect your
85 ensuing marriage—surely suit ill spent, and labour ill
bestowed.

Don Pedro
Why, what's the matter?

Don John
I came hither to tell you; and, circumstances
shortened—for she has been too long a talking of—
90 the lady is disloyal.

Claudio
Who, Hero?

Don John
Even she—Leonato's Hero, your Hero, every man's
Hero.

Claudio
Disloyal?

Don John
95 The word is too good to paint out her wickedness; I
could say she were worse. Think you of a worse title,
and I will fit her to it. Wonder not till further
warrant. Go but with me tonight, you shall see her
chamber window entered, even the night before her
100 wedding day. If you love her then, tomorrow wed
her. But it would better fit your honour to change
your mind.

Claudio
May this be so?

Don Pedro
I will not think it.

Don John
105 If you dare not trust that you see, confess not that
you know. If you will follow me I will show you

82-3 *aim . . . manifest*: judge me better
from what I will now reveal to you.
83 *holds you well*: thinks highly of you.
84 *holp*: helped.

88-9 *circumstances shortened*: cutting a long
story short.

95 *paint out*: give a full picture of.

105-6 *If you . . . know*: if you don't believe
what you see, say you don't know
anything (i.e. any reason why you
should not be married to Hero—see
4, 1, 11-13 *note*).

enough, and when you have seen more and heard more, proceed accordingly.

Claudio

If I see anything tonight why I should not marry her,
110 tomorrow, in the congregation where I should wed, there will I shame her.

Don Pedro

And as I wooed for thee to obtain her, I will join with thee to disgrace her.

Don John

I will disparage her no farther till you are my
115 witnesses. Bear it coldly but till midnight, and let the issue show itself.

Don Pedro

O day untowardly turned!

Claudio

O mischief strangely thwarting!

Don John

O plague right well prevented! So will you say when
120 you have seen the sequel.   [*Exeunt*

115 *coldly*: calmly.

117 *untowardly turned*: miserably transformed.

Act 3   Scene 3

The Watchmen, instructed to guard the city, overhear Borachio telling Conrad how Hero has been betrayed. An arrest is made.

os.d. *the Watch*: A number of citizens conscripted for (unpaid) police duty.

3   *salvation*: Verges means 'damnation'; such malapropisms form the characteristic speech modes of both Verges and Dogberry.

7   *charge*: duties.

8   *desertless*: Dogberry intends 'deserving'.

9   *constable*: officer responsible for maintenance of public order.

10 ***A Watchman***: Neither of the early texts distinguishes in speech-prefixes between the different Watchmen—whose number would vary according to the number of available actors.

Scene 3

Enter Dogberry *and his partner* Verges, *with the* Watch

Dogberry
Are you good men and true?

Verges
Yea, or else it were pity but they should suffer salvation, body and soul.

Dogberry
Nay, that were a punishment too good for them if
5 they should have any allegiance in them, being chosen for the prince's watch.

Verges
Well, give them their charge, neighbour Dogberry.

Dogberry
First, who think you the most desertless man to be constable?

A Watchman
10 Hugh Oatcake, sir, or George Seacoal, for they can write and read.

13 *well-favoured*: good looking.

14–15 *fortune . . . nature*: Dogberry seems to be trying to oppose the concepts of 'nature' and 'nurture' popular in philosophical discussion.

Dogberry
Come hither, neighbour Seacoal, God hath blessed you with a good name. To be a well-favoured man is the gift of fortune, but to write and read comes by
15 nature.
A Watchman
Both which, Master Constable—
Dogberry
You have. I knew it would be your answer. Well, for your favour, sir, why, give God thanks, and make no boast of it. And for your writing and reading, let that
20 appear when there is no need of such vanity. You are thought here to be the most senseless and fit man for the constable of the watch; therefore, bear you the lantern. This is your charge: you shall comprehend all vagrom men. You are to bid any man stand, in the
25 prince's name.

24 *vagrom*: vagrant.
    stand: halt.

A Watchman
How if a will not stand?

26 *a*: he.

Dogberry
Why then take no note of him, but let him go, and presently call the rest of the watch together, and thank God you are rid of a knave.
Verges
30 If he will not stand when he is bidden, he is none of the prince's subjects.
Dogberry
True, and they are to meddle with none but the prince's subjects. You shall also make no noise in the streets, for for the watch to babble and to talk is most
35 tolerable and not to be endured.

32 *meddle*: be concerned with.

A Watchman
We will rather sleep than talk. We know what belongs to a watch.
Dogberry
Why, you speak like an ancient and most quiet watchman, for I cannot see how sleeping should
40 offend. Only have a care that your bills be not stolen. Well, you are to call at all the alehouses and bid those that are drunk get them to bed.

38 *ancient*: experienced.

40 *bills*: halberds (long-handled, axe-headed weapons).

A Watchman
How if they will not?

49 *true*: honest.

54 5 *they . . . defiled*: Dogberry quotes from
the Apocrypha (Ecclesiasticus 13:1).

59 *by my will*: if I had my way.

65–6 *the ewe . . . bleats*: Dogberry seems to
invent his own folk wisdom.

69 *present*: represent.

Dogberry
Why then, let them alone till they are sober. If they
45 make you not then the better answer, you may say
they are not the men you took them for.
A Watchman
Well, sir.
Dogberry
If you meet a thief you may suspect him, by virtue of
your office, to be no true man; and for such kind of
50 men, the less you meddle or make with them, why,
the more is for your honesty.
A Watchman
If we know him to be a thief, shall we not lay hands
on him?
Dogberry
Truly, by your office you may, but I think they that
55 touch pitch will be defiled. The most peaceable way
for you if you do take a thief is to let him show
himself what he is, and steal out of your company.
Verges
You have been always called a merciful man, partner.
Dogberry
Truly, I would not hang a dog by my will, much
60 more a man who hath any honesty in him.
Verges
If you hear a child cry in the night, you must call to
the nurse and bid her still it.
A Watchman
How if the nurse be asleep and will not hear us?
Dogberry
Why then, depart in peace and let the child wake her
65 with crying, for the ewe that will not hear her lamb
when it baas will never answer a calf when he bleats.
Verges
'Tis very true.
Dogberry
This is the end of the charge. You, constable, are to
present the prince's own person. If you meet the
70 prince in the night you may stay him.
Verges
Nay, by'r Lady, that I think a cannot.

Dogberry

Five shillings to one on't with any man that knows
the statutes he may stay him. Marry, not without the
prince be willing, for indeed the watch ought to
75 offend no man, and it is an offence to stay a man
against his will.

Verges

By'r Lady, I think it be so.

Dogberry

Ha ha ha! Well, masters, good night. An there be any
matter of weight chances, call up me. Keep your
80 fellows' counsels, and your own, and good night. [*To
Verges*] Come, neighbour.

A Watchman

Well, masters, we hear our charge. Let us go sit here
upon the church bench till two, and then all to bed.

Dogberry

One word more, honest neighbours. I pray you
85 watch about Signor Leonato's door, for the wedding
being there tomorrow, there is a great coil tonight.
Adieu. Be vigitant, I beseech you.

[*Exeunt* Dogberry *and* Verges

Enter Borachio *and* Conrad

Borachio

What, Conrad!

A Watchman

[*Aside*] Peace, stir not.

Borachio

90 Conrad, I say.

Conrad

Here, man, I am at thy elbow.

Borachio

Mass, an my elbow itched, I thought there would a
scab follow.

Conrad

I will owe thee an answer for that. And now, forward
95 with thy tale.

78 *Ha ha ha*: Dogberry has forced Verges
to agree with him
An: if.

86 *coil*: commotion, bustle.
87 *vigitant*: vigilant.

92 *Mass*: by the mass (a mild oath).
my elbow itched: This was proverbially
said to be a warning of evil or danger.
93 *scab*: scoundrel—and the result of
scratching the itch.

96 *penthouse*: overhang (probably the
   projection above part of the stage).
97 *a true drunkard*: i.e. truthfully (*in vino
   veritas*—there's truth in wine).

99 *close*: hidden.
101 *thousand ducats*: The sum was large, but
    not enormous; the ducat varied in value
    at different times and in different
    countries.
105 *make*: ask.
108 *unconfirmed*: inexperienced.
109–10 *is nothing . . . man*: tells you nothing
    about a man (but Conrad understands
    'means nothing *to* a man').
115 *deformed*: perverse, absurd.

Borachio
Stand thee close then under this penthouse, for it
drizzles rain; and I will, like a true drunkard, utter all
to thee.

A Watchman
[*Aside*] Some treason, masters. Yet stand close.

Borachio
100 Therefore, know I have earned of Don John a
thousand ducats.

Conrad
Is it possible that any villainy should be so dear?

Borachio
Thou shouldst rather ask if it were possible any
villainy should be so rich. For when rich villains have
105 need of poor ones, poor ones may make what price
they will.

Conrad
I wonder at it.

Borachio
That shows thou art unconfirmed. Thou knowest
that the fashion of a doublet, or a hat, or a cloak is
110 nothing to a man.

Conrad
Yes, it is apparel.

Borachio
I mean the fashion.

Conrad
Yes, the fashion is the fashion.

Borachio
Tush, I may as well say the fool's the fool. But seest
115 thou not what a deformed thief this fashion is?

A Watchman
[*Aside*] I know that Deformed. A has been a vile thief
this seven year. A goes up and down like a
gentleman. I remember his name.

Borachio
Didst thou not hear somebody?

Conrad
120 No, 'twas the vane on the house.

Borachio
Seest thou not, I say, what a deformed thief this
fashion is, how giddily a turns about all the hot-

124–5 *Pharaoh's . . . painting*: Borachio refers
to a wall-hanging in some tavern;
Pharaoh's soldiers were drowned in the
Red Sea when they were pursuing
Moses and the Israelites (Exodus
14:23–8).

125   *reechy*: grimy.
      god Bel's priests: The priests were slain
      by the king of Persia after Daniel
      denounced them for worshipping a false
      god (Apocrypha: The Book of Daniel,
      chapter 14, Douai Bible).
126–8 *shaven Hercules . . . club*: Borachio
      perhaps refers to a picture of Hercules
      with Omphale (see *2, 1, 234–6 note*),
      although Hercules never lost his beard.
128   *codpiece*: decorative pouch worn at the
      front of a man's breeches.
131   *shifted*: changed (with a pun on shift =
      change clothes).
139   *possessed by*: convinced by, under the
      [diabolic] influence of.
146   *my villainy*: Borachio must have been
      questioned by Don Pedro and Claudio
      after his performance.
155   *lechery*: for 'treachery'.

bloods   between   fourteen   and   five-and-thirty,
sometimes fashioning them like Pharaoh's soldiers in
125 the reechy painting, sometime like god Bel's priests
in the old church window, sometime like the shaven
Hercules   in   the   smirched,   worm-eaten   tapestry,
where his codpiece seems as massy as his club?

Conrad

All this I see, and I see that the fashion wears out
130 more apparel than the man. But art not thou thyself
giddy with the fashion, too, that thou hast shifted
out of thy tale into telling me of the fashion?

Borachio

Not so, neither. But know that I have tonight wooed
Margaret, the Lady Hero's gentlewoman, by the
135 name of Hero. She leans me out at her mistress'
chamber window, bids me a thousand times good
night.—I tell this tale vilely. I should first tell thee
how the prince, Claudio, and my master, planted
and placed and possessed by my master Don John,
140 saw afar off in the orchard this amiable encounter.

Conrad

And thought they Margaret was Hero?

Borachio

Two of them did, the prince and Claudio. But the
devil my master knew she was Margaret. And partly
by his oaths, which first possessed them, partly by
145 the dark night, which did deceive them, but chiefly
by my villainy, which did confirm any slander that
Don John had made—away went Claudio enraged,
swore he would meet her as he was appointed next
morning at the temple, and there, before the whole
150 congregation, shame her with what he saw o'ernight,
and send her home again without a husband.

A Watchman

[*Coming forward*] We charge you in the prince's
name. Stand!

A Watchman

Call up the right Master Constable. We have here
155 recovered the most dangerous piece of lechery that
ever was known in the commonwealth.

158 *lock*: lovelock, hanging curl (a
fashionable hairstyle at the time).

165 *commodity*: useful article, *and*, goods
obtained on credit.
taken up: received on credit, arrested.
bills: halberds, security bonds.
166 *in question*: in demand, questionable
(legally).

A Watchman
And one Deformed is one of them. I know him; a
wears a lock.
    Conrad
Masters, masters—
    A Watchman
160 You'll be made bring Deformed forth, I warrant you.
    Conrad
Masters—
    A Watchman
Never speak, we charge you. Let us obey you to go
with us.
    Borachio
[*To* Conrad] We are like to prove a goodly
165 commodity, being taken up of these men's bills.
    Conrad
A commodity in question, I warrant you. Come,
we'll obey you.   [*Exeunt*

Act 3   Scene 4

Hero is being dressed for her wedding—but
Beatrice has a heavy cold.

6 *Troth*: faith.
rebato: a stiff ornamented collar pinned
on to a lady's gown.

Scene 4

Enter Hero, Margaret, *and* Ursula

    Hero
Good Ursula, wake my cousin Beatrice, and desire
her to rise.
    Ursula
I will, lady.
    Hero
And bid her come hither.
    Ursula
5 Well.   [*Exit*
    Margaret
Troth, I think your other rebato were better.
    Hero
No, pray thee, good Meg, I'll wear this.
    Margaret
By my troth, 's not so good, and I warrant your
cousin will say so.

12 *tire*: decorative head-dress (perhaps incorporating false hair and ornaments).

16 *exceeds*: beats everything.

17 *night-gown*: dressing-gown; these were often very elaborate creations of silk or satin, trimmed with fur.

18 *cuts*: slashes in the main fabric of a gown revealing even richer cloth beneath.

19 *down . . . sleeves*: tight sleeves fitted down to the wrist, and looser, fuller sleeves draped from the shoulders.

20 *underborne*: trimmed at the hem, or worn over a petticoat.
bluish tinsel: light blue silk cloth shot through with gold or silver threads.

21 *quaint*: intricate and elegant.

Hero

10 My cousin's a fool, and thou art another; I'll wear none but this.

Margaret

I like the new tire within excellently, if the hair were a thought browner. And your gown's a most rare fashion, i' faith. I saw the Duchess of Milan's gown

15 that they praise so.

Hero

O, that exceeds, they say.

Margaret

By my troth, 's but a night-gown in respect of yours—cloth o' gold, and cuts, and laced with silver, set with pearls, down sleeves, side sleeves, and skirts

20 round underborne with a bluish tinsel. But for a fine, quaint, graceful, and excellent fashion, yours is worth ten on't.

Hero

God give me joy to wear it, for my heart is exceeding heavy.

Margaret

25 'Twill be heavier soon by the weight of a man.

Hero

Fie upon thee, art not ashamed?

Margaret

Of what, lady? Of speaking honourably? Is not marriage honourable in a beggar? Is not your lord

29 *honourable*: 'holy Matrimony . . . is an
   honourable estate' ('Order for the
   Solemnization of Matrimony' in *The
   Book of Common Prayer*).
30 *saving your reverence*: if you don't mind
   me saying so.
30-1 *An . . . speaking*: i.e. 'if your dirty
   mind doesn't twist my words'.
34 *light*: wanton, promiscuous.

36 *coz*: a term of endearment (= cousin).

38 *sick*: sad.

40 *Clap 's . . . love'*: let's sing a round of
   'Light o' love'—a popular song (the
   words are unknown) whose rhythm
   could be started by clapping.
41 *burden*: bass part for male voices.
42 *light o' love*: wanton, promiscuous.
44 *barns*: bairns (= babies).

45 *illegitimate construction*: false
   interpretation (with obvious double
   meaning).
45-6 *with my heels*: by kicking backwards
   (like a horse).

49 *Heigh-ho*: Beatrice sighs.

51 *h*: ache (then, like the letter,
   pronounced 'aitch').
52 *an*: if.
   turned Turk: changed faith; the phrase
   was proverbial.
53 *the star*: i.e. the Pole Star, navigational
   fixed point.
54 *trow*: do you know, I wonder.
55-6 *God . . . desire*: 'Delight thou in the
   Lord: and he shall give thee thy heart's
   desire' (Psalm 37:4 in the *Book of
   Common Prayer*).

---

honourable without marriage? I think you would
30 have me say 'saving your reverence, a husband'. An
bad thinking do not wrest true speaking, I'll offend
nobody. Is there any harm in 'the heavier for a
husband'? None, I think, an it be the right husband
and the right wife; otherwise 'tis light and not heavy.
35 Ask my Lady Beatrice else. Here she comes.

Enter Beatrice

Hero
Good morrow, coz.
Beatrice
Good morrow, sweet Hero.
Hero
Why, how now? Do you speak in the sick tune?
Beatrice
I am out of all other tune, methinks.
Margaret
40 Clap 's into 'Light o' love'; that goes without a
burden. Do you sing it, and I'll dance it.
Beatrice
Ye light o' love with your heels! Then if your
husband have stables enough, you'll see he shall lack
no barns.
Margaret
45 O illegitimate construction! I scorn that with my
heels.
Beatrice
[*To* Hero] 'Tis almost five o'clock, cousin. 'Tis time
you were ready. By my troth, I am exceeding ill.
Heigh-ho!
Margaret
50 For a hawk, a horse, or a husband?
Beatrice
For the letter that begins them all—h.
Margaret
Well, an you be not turned Turk, there's no more
sailing by the star.
Beatrice
What means the fool, trow?
Margaret
55 Nothing, I. But God send everyone their heart's
desire.

57 *are*: have.
58 *perfume*: Gloves were usually perfumed to disguise the smell of the leather.

59 *am stuffed*: have a cold in the head—but Margaret is quick to hear innuendo.

63 *professed apprehension*: prided yourself on your wit.

65 *rarely*: splendidly; Beatrice understands 'infrequently'.

66 *in your cap*: i.e. as a fool wears a coxcomb.

68 *carduus benedictus*: 'holy thistle', a popular remedy for all ailments.
69 *qualm*: sudden nausea.

70 *prick'st . . . thistle*: Hero seems to have joined in with the other girls' bawdy jokes.

73–85 *Moral . . . do*: Margaret talks nonsense to divert Beatrice's suspicion.
74 *plain*: simply, literally.
75 *by'r Lady*: by Our Lady (the Virgin Mary).
76 *list*: please.

82–3 *in despite . . . grudging*: 'even though he's in love, he doesn't make such a fuss about it'.

86 *What . . . keeps*: whatever are you trying to say.
87 *Not . . . gallop*: nothing that's not true; a 'false gallop' was only a rapid canter.

Hero
These gloves the count sent me, they are an excellent perfume.

Beatrice
I am stuffed, cousin; I cannot smell.

Margaret
60 A maid, and stuffed! There's goodly catching of cold.

Beatrice
O, God help me, God help me. How long have you professed apprehension?

Margaret
Ever since you left it. Doth not my wit become me
65 rarely?

Beatrice
It is not seen enough. You should wear it in your cap. By my troth, I am sick.

Margaret
Get you some of this distilled *carduus benedictus*, and lay it to your heart. It is the only thing for a qualm.

Hero
70 There thou prick'st her with a thistle.

Beatrice
Benedictus—why *benedictus*? You have some moral in this *benedictus*.

Margaret
Moral? No, by my troth, I have no moral meaning. I meant plain holy-thistle. You may think perchance
75 that I think you are in love. Nay, by'r Lady, I am not such a fool to think what I list. Nor I list not to think what I can, nor indeed I cannot think—if I would think my heart out of thinking—that you are in love, or that you will be in love, or that you can be in love.
80 Yet Benedick was such another, and now is he become a man. He swore he would never marry, and yet now in despite of his heart he eats his meat without grudging. And how you may be converted I know not, but methinks you look with your eyes, as
85 other women do.

Beatrice
What pace is this that thy tongue keeps?

Margaret
Not a false gallop.

Enter Ursula

Ursula
[*To* Hero] Madam, withdraw. The prince, the count,
Signor Benedick, Don John, and all the gallants of
90 the town are come to fetch you to church.
Hero
Help to dress me, good coz, good Meg, good Ursula.
                                        [*Exeunt*

Act 3   Scene 5

Dogberry reports his arrest to Leonato, who is too busy to listen to him.

2 *confidence*: confidential conference; this time Dogberry means what he says.
3 *decerns*: concerns.

Scene 5

Enter Leonato, Dogberry *the constable, and*
Verges *the Headborough*

Leonato
What would you with me, honest neighbour?
Dogberry
Marry, sir, I would have some confidence with you
that decerns you nearly.
Leonato
Brief, I pray you, for you see it is a busy time with
5 me.

Dogberry
Marry, this it is, sir.

Verges
Yes, in truth it is, sir.

Leonato
What is it, my good friends?

Dogberry
Goodman Verges, sir, speaks a little off the matter—
10 an old man, sir, and his wits are not so blunt as, God
help, I would desire they were. But in faith, honest as
the skin between his brows.

Verges
Yes, I thank God, I am as honest as any man living
that is an old man and no honester than I.

Dogberry
15 Comparisons are odorous. '*Palabras*', neighbour
Verges.

Leonato
Neighbours, you are tedious.

Dogberry
It pleases your worship to say so, but we are the poor
duke's officers. But truly, for mine own part, if I were
20 as tedious as a king I could find in my heart to
bestow it all of your worship.

Leonato
All thy tediousness on me, ah?

Dogberry
Yea, an 'twere a thousand pound more than 'tis, for
I hear as good exclamation on your worship as of any
25 man in the city, and though I be but a poor man, I
am glad to hear it.

Verges
And so am I.

Leonato
I would fain know what you have to say.

Verges
Marry, sir, our watch tonight, excepting your
30 worship's presence, ha' ta'en a couple of as arrant
knaves as any in Messina.

Dogberry
A good old man, sir. He will be talking. As they say,
when the age is in, the wit is out. God help us, it is a
world to see. Well said, i' faith, neighbour Verges.

11–12 *honest . . . brows*: The expression was
proverbial.

15 *odorous*: i.e. 'odious'.
Palabras: The Spanish expression '*pocas
palabras*' (= few words) was popular at
this time.

17 *tedious*: Dogberry takes this for flattery
(perhaps meaning 'generous').

24 *exclamation*: i.e. 'acclamation'.

33 *when . . . out*: Dogberry garbles the
proverb 'When *ale* is in, wit is out'.

35 Well, God's a good man. An two men ride of a horse, one must ride behind. An honest soul, i' faith, sir, by my troth he is, as ever broke bread. But God is to be worshipped; all men are not alike, alas, good neighbour.

Leonato

40 Indeed, neighbour, he comes too short of you.

Dogberry

Gifts that God gives!

Leonato

I must leave you.

Dogberry

One word, sir. Our watch, sir, have indeed comprehended two auspicious persons, and we

45 would have them this morning examined before your worship.

Leonato

Take their examination yourself, and bring it me. I am now in great haste, as it may appear unto you.

Dogberry

It shall be suffigance.

Leonato

50 Drink some wine ere you go. Fare you well.

Enter a Messenger

Messenger

My lord, they stay for you to give your daughter to her husband.

Leonato

I'll wait upon them, I am ready.

[*Exeunt* Leonato *and* Messenger

Dogberry

Go, good partner, go get you to Francis Seacoal. Bid

55 him bring his pen and inkhorn to the jail. We are now to examination these men.

Verges

And we must do it wisely.

Dogberry

We will spare for no wit, I warrant you. Here's that shall drive some of them to a non-com. Only get the

60 learned writer to set down our excommunication, and meet me at the jail.

[*Exeunt*

40 *comes . . . you*: isn't your equal.

44 *comprehended*: i.e. 'apprehended'. *auspicious*: i.e. 'suspicious'.

49 *suffigance*: sufficient.

58 *that*: Dogberry indicates his head.

59 *non-com*: Perhaps Dogberry intends 'nonplus' (= bafflement, perplexity) but in fact his expression suggests '*non compos mentis*' (= out of their minds).

Act 4

Act 4   Scene 1

The wedding party assembles and Claudio denounces Hero—who faints with the shock. The friar has a scheme to make all well, and Benedick offers his services to Beatrice with his love—which she accepts and returns.

1–2 *plain form*: simple formalities (without lengthy sermonizing).
11–13 *If either . . . utter it*: 'if either of you know any impediment, why you may not be lawfully joined together in Matrimony, you do now confess it' ('Order for the Solemnization of Matrimony' in *The Book of Common Prayer*).

11 *inward*: secret.

Scene 1

Enter Don Pedro *the prince*, Don John *the bastard*, Leonato, Friar Francis, Claudio, Benedick, Hero, *and* Beatrice, *with* Guests *and* Attendants

Leonato
Come, Friar Francis, be brief. Only to the plain form of marriage, and you shall recount their particular duties afterwards.

Friar
[*To* Claudio] You come hither, my lord, to marry this
5 lady?

Claudio
No.

Leonato
To be married to her. Friar, you come to marry her.

Friar
[*To* Hero] Lady, you come hither to be married to this count?

Hero
10 I do.

Friar
If either of you know any inward impediment why you should not be conjoined, I charge you on your souls to utter it.

Claudio
Know you any, Hero?

Hero
15 None, my lord.

Friar
Know you any, Count?

Leonato

I dare make his answer—none.

Claudio

O, what men dare do! What men may do! What men daily do, not knowing what they do!

Benedick

20 How now! Interjections? Why then, some be of laughing, as 'ah, ha, he!'

Claudio

Stand thee by, Friar. [*To* Leonato] Father, by your leave,

Will you with free and unconstrained soul

Give me this maid, your daughter?

Leonato

25 As freely, son, as God did give her me.

Claudio

And what have I to give you back whose worth

May counterpoise this rich and precious gift?

Don Pedro

Nothing, unless you render her again.

Claudio

Sweet Prince, you learn me noble thankfulness.

30 There, Leonato, take her back again.

Give not this rotten orange to your friend!

She's but the sign and semblance of her honour.

Behold how like a maid she blushes here.

O, what authority and show of truth

35 Can cunning sin cover itself withal!

Comes not that blood as modest evidence

To witness simple virtue? Would you not swear—

All you that see her—that she were a maid,

By these exterior shows? But she is none.

40 She knows the heat of a luxurious bed.

Her blush is guiltiness, not modesty.

Leonato

What do you mean, my lord?

Claudio

                         Not to be married,

Not to knit my soul to an approved wanton.

Leonato

Dear my lord, if you in your own proof

45 Have vanquish'd the resistance of her youth

And made defeat of her virginity—

20–1 *some . . . he*: Benedick quotes William Lyly's Latin grammar, a standard school text: 'Some [interjections] are of . . . laughing: as *Ha, ha, he.*'

22 *by your leave*: if I may so call you.

23 *unconstrained*: unconstrainèd.

24 *maid*: virgin.

29 *learn*: teach.

37 *witness*: give evidence of.

40 *luxurious*: lustful.

43 *approved*: approvèd; proven.

44 *in . . . proof*: to test it for yourself.

47 *known*: had intercourse with.

48–9 *embrace . . . sin*: The formal engagement of 2, 1, 280–2 constitutes a legally valid 'marriage by pre-contract'—which would permit such 'forehand' embracing.

51 *word . . . large*: improper suggestions.

55 *Out on*: that's enough of.
write against: denounce.

56 *Dian . . . orb*: Diana, the chaste goddess of the moon.

57 *blown*: fully opened.

59 *Venus*: goddess of desire and sexual love.
those pamper'd animals: horses (believed by the Elizabethans to be sexually over-active).

61 *wide*: wide of the mark, inaccurately.

64 *stale*: whore.

73 *kindly power*: power of kinship.

Claudio
I know what you would say. If I have known her,
You will say she did embrace me as a husband,
And so extenuate the forehand sin.
50 No, Leonato,
I never tempted her with word too large,
But as a brother to his sister show'd
Bashful sincerity and comely love.

Hero
And seem'd I ever otherwise to you?

Claudio
55 Out on thy seeming! I will write against it.
You seem to me as Dian in her orb,
As chaste as is the bud ere it be blown.
But you are more intemperate in your blood
Than Venus or those pamper'd animals
60 That rage in savage sensuality.

Hero
Is my lord well that he doth speak so wide?

Leonato
Sweet Prince, why speak not you?

Don Pedro
                              What should I speak?
I stand dishonour'd, that have gone about
To link my dear friend to a common stale.

Leonato
65 Are these things spoken, or do I but dream?

Don John
Sir, they are spoken, and these things are true.

Benedick
This looks not like a nuptial.

Hero
                              True? O God!

Claudio
Leonato, stand I here?
Is this the prince? Is this the prince's brother?
70 Is this face Hero's? Are our eyes our own?

Leonato
All this is so. But what of this, my lord?

Claudio
Let me but move one question to your daughter,
And by that fatherly and kindly power
That you have in her, bid her answer truly.

77 *catechizing*: Elizabethan children were
taught their religion by a question-and-
answer catechism which began 'What is
your name?'
78 *answer . . . name*: acknowledge that you
are what we have called you (i.e.
unchaste).

88 *grieved*: grievèd; wronged.

91 *liberal*: licentious.

97 *misgovernment*: misconduct.

103 *gates of love*: the senses (especially the
eyes).
104 *conjecture*: suspicion.

Leonato

75 [*To* Hero] I charge thee do so, as thou art my child.

Hero

O God defend me! How am I beset!
What kind of catechizing call you this?

Claudio

To make you answer truly to your name.

Hero

Is it not Hero? Who can blot that name
80 With any just reproach?

Claudio

                              Marry, that can Hero.
Hero itself can blot out Hero's virtue.
What man was he talk'd with you yesternight
Out at your window betwixt twelve and one?
Now, if you are a maid, answer to this.

Hero

85 I talk'd with no man at that hour, my lord.

Don Pedro

Why, then are you no maiden. Leonato,
I am sorry you must hear. Upon mine honour,
Myself, my brother, and this grieved count
Did see her, hear her, at that hour last night
90 Talk with a ruffian at her chamber window,
Who hath indeed, most like a liberal villain,
Confess'd the vile encounters they have had
A thousand times in secret.

Don John

                              Fie, fie, they are
Not to be nam'd, my lord, not to be spoke of.
95 There is not chastity enough in language
Without offence to utter them. Thus, pretty lady,
I am sorry for thy much misgovernment.

Claudio

O Hero! What a Hero hadst thou been
If half thy outward graces had been plac'd
100 About thy thoughts and counsels of thy heart!
But fare thee well, most foul, most fair; farewell
Thou pure impiety and impious purity.
For thee I'll lock up all the gates of love,
And on my eyelids shall conjecture hang
105 To turn all beauty into thoughts of harm,
And never shall it more be gracious.

Leonato
Hath no man's dagger here a point for me?

Hero *falls to the ground*

Beatrice
Why, how now, cousin, wherefore sink you down?
Don John
Come, let us go. These things come thus to light
110 Smother her spirits up.
        [*Exeunt* Don Pedro, Don John, *and* Claudio
Benedick
How doth the lady?
Beatrice
               Dead, I think. Help, uncle.
Hero, why Hero! Uncle, Signor Benedick, Friar—
Leonato
O Fate, take not away thy heavy hand.
Death is the fairest cover for her shame
115 That may be wish'd for.
Beatrice
                How now, cousin Hero?
Friar
Have comfort, lady.
Leonato
Dost thou look up?
Friar
Yea, wherefore should she not?
Leonato
Wherefore? Why, doth not every earthly thing
120 Cry shame upon her? Could she here deny
The story that is printed in her blood?
Do not live, Hero, do not ope thine eyes;
For did I think thou wouldst not quickly die,
Thought I thy spirits were stronger than thy shames,
125 Myself would, on the rearward of reproaches,
Strike at thy life. Griev'd I, I had but one?
Chid I for that at frugal nature's frame?
O one too much by thee! Why had I one?
Why ever wast thou lovely in my eyes?
130 Why had I not with charitable hand
Took up a beggar's issue at my gates,
Who, smirched thus, and mir'd with infamy,
I might have said 'No part of it is mine;

110 *spirits*: the vital powers controlling bodily functions.

117 *look up*: i.e. to heaven (imploring aid).

121 *printed . . . blood*: shown in her blushes of shame, stamped on her life.

125 *on the rearward of*: immediately after.

127 *frame*: plan.

131 *issue*: child.
132 *smirched*: smirchèd.

135-7 *mine . . . mine*: i.e. 'I cared so much for my child that I took no care of myself.'

This shame derives itself from unknown loins.'
135 But mine, and mine I lov'd, and mine I prais'd,
And mine that I was proud on; mine so much
That I myself was to myself not mine,
Valuing of her—why she, O she is fallen
Into a pit of ink, that the wide sea
140 Hath drops too few to wash her clean again,
And salt too little which may season give
To her foul, tainted flesh.

141 *salt . . . season*: The Elizabethans used salt to preserve their meat.

Benedick
                                    Sir, sir, be patient.
For my part, I am so attir'd in wonder
I know not what to say.

Beatrice
145 O, on my soul, my cousin is belied.

Benedick
Lady, were you her bedfellow last night?

146 *bedfellow*: It was usual in Elizabethan days for two adults of the same sex to share a bed.

Beatrice
No, truly not, although until last night
I have this twelvemonth been her bedfellow.

Leonato
Confirm'd, confirm'd. O, that is stronger made
150 Which was before barr'd up with ribs of iron.
Would the two princes lie? And Claudio lie,
Who lov'd her so that, speaking of her foulness,
Wash'd it with tears? Hence from her, let her die.

Friar
Hear me a little,

153 *tears*: Claudio perhaps shed tears of disappointed rage when he accused Hero.
159 *shames*: embarrassments.
163 *maiden truth*: the truth of her virginity.
165 *experimental seal*: validation of experience.
165-6 *warrant . . . book*: confirm the substance of my reading.

155 For I have only silent been so long
And given way unto this course of fortune.
By noting of the lady, I have mark'd
A thousand blushing apparitions
To start into her face, a thousand innocent shames
160 In angel whiteness beat away those blushes,
And in her eye there hath appear'd a fire
To burn the errors that these princes hold
Against her maiden truth. Call me a fool,
Trust not my reading nor my observations,
165 Which with experimental seal doth warrant
The tenor of my book. Trust not my age,
My reverence, calling, nor divinity,
If this sweet lady lie not guiltless here
Under some biting error.

Leonato

                               Friar, it cannot be.

170 Thou seest that all the grace that she hath left
    Is that she will not add to her damnation
    A sin of perjury. She not denies it.
    Why seek'st thou then to cover with excuse
    That which appears in proper nakedness?

Friar

175 Lady, what man is he you are accus'd of?

Hero

    They know that do accuse me; I know none.
    If I know more of any man alive
    Than that which maiden modesty doth warrant,
    Let all my sins lack mercy. O my father,

180 Prove you that any man with me convers'd
    At hours unmeet, or that I yesternight
    Maintain'd the change of words with any creature,
    Refuse me, hate me, torture me to death.

Friar

    There is some strange misprision in the princes.

Benedick

185 Two of them have the very bent of honour,
    And if their wisdoms be misled in this
    The practice of it lives in John the Bastard,
    Whose spirits toil in frame of villainies.

Leonato

    I know not. If they speak but truth of her,

190 These hands shall tear her. If they wrong her
      honour,
    The proudest of them shall well hear of it.
    Time hath not yet so dried this blood of mine,
    Nor age so eat up my invention,
    Nor fortune made such havoc of my means,

195 Nor my bad life reft me so much of friends,
    But they shall find awak'd in such a kind
    Both strength of limb and policy of mind,
    Ability in means, and choice of friends,
    To quit me of them throughly.

Friar

                              Pause a while,

200 And let my counsel sway you in this case.
    Your daughter here the princes left for dead.

---

174 *proper*: natural, undisguised.

181 *unmeet*: improper.

184 *misprision*: misunderstanding.

185 *the very bent of*: the right inclination to.

187 *practice*: trickery.
John the Bastard: This is the first time any of the characters has given this description.

188 *frame*: designing.

193 *invention*: resourcefulness. The word here is pronounced with four syllables.

195 *reft*: bereft.

197 *policy*: ingenuity.

199 *quit . . . throughly*: pay them back in full.

202 *in*: at home.

204 *mourning ostentation*: show of mourning.
205 *monument*: burial vault.

212 *travail*: labour.

216 *Of*: by.
217 *not . . . worth*: as much as it is worth.

219 *rack*: stretch out, exaggerate.

224 *his . . . imagination*: his pensive thoughts.
225 *organ*: aspect.
226 *habit*: attire.
227 *moving*: affecting.

230 *had interest in*: had any part of.
    liver: This was thought to be the seat of love.
231 *accused*: accusèd.
233 *success*: succeeding events.
234 *event*: outcome.

236 *if . . . false*: if we miss our aim in every other respect but this.

238 *wonder*: gossip.
239 *sort*: turn out.

241 *reclusive*: cloistered.

Let her a while be secretly kept in,
And publish it that she is dead indeed.
Maintain a mourning ostentation,
205 And on your family's old monument
Hang mournful epitaphs, and do all rites
That appertain unto a burial.
Leonato
What shall become of this? What will this do?
Friar
Marry, this, well carried, shall on her behalf
210 Change slander to remorse. That is some good.
But not for that dream I on this strange course,
But on this travail look for greater birth.
She dying—as it must be so maintain'd—
Upon the instant that she was accus'd,
215 Shall be lamented, pitied, and excus'd
Of every hearer. For it so falls out
That what we have we prize not to the worth
Whiles we enjoy it, but being lack'd and lost,
Why, then we rack the value, then we find
220 The virtue that possession would not show us
Whiles it was ours. So will it fare with Claudio.
When he shall hear she died upon his words,
Th'idea of her life shall sweetly creep
Into his study of imagination,
225 And every lovely organ of her life
Shall come apparell'd in more precious habit,
More moving, delicate, and full of life,
Into the eye and prospect of his soul
Than when she liv'd indeed. Then shall he mourn,
230 If ever love had interest in his liver,
And wish he had not so accused her—
No, though he thought his accusation true.
Let this be so, and doubt not but success
Will fashion the event in better shape
235 Than I can lay it down in likelihood.
But if all aim but this be levell'd false,
The supposition of the lady's death
Will quench the wonder of her infamy.
And if it sort not well, you may conceal her,
240 As best befits her wounded reputation,
In some reclusive and religious life,

Out of all eyes, tongues, minds, and injuries.

Benedick

Signor Leonato, let the friar advise you;

And though you know my inwardness and love

245 Is very much unto the prince and Claudio,

Yet, by mine honour, I will deal in this

As secretly and justly as your soul

Should with your body.

Leonato

Being that I flow in grief,

The smallest twine may lead me.

Friar

250 'Tis well consented. Presently away,

For to strange sores strangely they strain the cure.

[*To* Hero] Come, lady, die to live. This wedding day

Perhaps is but prolong'd. Have patience and endure.

[*Exeunt all but* Beatrice *and* Benedick

Benedick

Lady Beatrice, have you wept all this while?

Beatrice

255 Yea, and I will weep a while longer.

Benedick

I will not desire that.

Beatrice

You have no reason; I do it freely.

Benedick

Surely I do believe your fair cousin is wronged.

Beatrice

Ah, how much might the man deserve of me that

260 would right her!

Benedick

Is there any way to show such friendship?

Beatrice

A very even way, but no such friend.

Benedick

May a man do it?

Beatrice

It is a man's office, but not yours.

Benedick

265 I do love nothing in the world so well as you. Is not

that strange?

244 *inwardness*: intimate friendship.

248 *flow in grief*: am overwhelmed by grief.
249 *twine*: thread.

251 *to strange . . . cure*: A proverbial saying: desperate diseases must have desperate cures.
253 *Perhaps . . . endure*: A line of 12 syllables (alexandrine) brings the episode to its close.
prolong'd: postponed.

262 *even*: direct.

264 *office*: task.

267 *the thing I know not*: I don't know what.

272 *By my sword*: The oath of a Christian gentleman, sworn on the cross made by the hilt of his weapon.

273 *eat it*: eat the sword—i.e. his words.

277 *protest*: declare.

279 *God forgive me*: i.e. for being about to flout convention and be the first to declare her love.

281 *stayed*: stopped, forestalled.
in a happy hour: at a propitious moment.

291 *I am gone . . . here*: 'I have gone in spirit, though I am held here by force.'

Beatrice

As strange as the thing I know not. It were as possible for me to say I loved nothing so well as you. But believe me not, and yet I lie not. I confess
270 nothing nor I deny nothing; I am sorry for my cousin.

Benedick

By my sword, Beatrice, thou lovest me.

Beatrice

Do not swear and eat it.

Benedick

I will swear by it that you love me, and I will make
275 him eat it that says I love not you.

Beatrice

Will you not eat your word?

Benedick

With no sauce that can be devised to it. I protest I love thee.

Beatrice

Why then, God forgive me.

Benedick

280 What offence, sweet Beatrice?

Beatrice

You have stayed me in a happy hour. I was about to protest I loved you.

Benedick

And do it with all thy heart.

Beatrice

I love you with so much of my heart that none is left
285 to protest.

Benedick

Come, bid me do anything for thee.

Beatrice

Kill Claudio.

Benedick

Ha! Not for the wide world.

Beatrice

You kill me to deny it. Farewell.

Benedick

290 [*Barring her way*] Tarry, sweet Beatrice.

Beatrice

I am gone though I am here. There is no love in you.—Nay, I pray you, let me go.

Benedick

Beatrice—

Beatrice

In faith, I will go.

Benedick

295 We'll be friends first.

Beatrice

You dare easier be friends with me than fight with mine enemy.

Benedick

Is Claudio thine enemy?

Beatrice

Is a not approved in the height a villain, that hath
300 slandered, scorned, dishonoured my kinswoman? O that I were a man! What, bear her in hand until they come to take hands, and then with public accusation, uncovered slander, unmitigated rancour—O God that I were a man! I would eat his
305 heart in the market place.

Benedick

Hear me, Beatrice—

Beatrice

Talk with a man out at a window—a proper saying!

Benedick

Nay, but Beatrice—

Beatrice

Sweet Hero! She is wronged, she is slandered, she is
310 undone.

Benedick

Beat—

Beatrice

Princes and counties! Surely a princely testimony, a goodly count; Count Comfit, a sweet gallant, surely. O that I were a man for his sake! Or that I had any
315 friend would be a man for my sake! But manhood is melted into curtsies, valour into compliment, and men are only turned into tongue, and trim ones, too. He is now as valiant as Hercules that only tells a lie and swears it. I cannot be a man with wishing;
320 therefore I will die a woman with grieving.

Benedick

Tarry, good Beatrice. By this hand, I love thee.

301 *bear . . . hand*: lead her on with false pretences.
302 *take hands*: join hands in marriage.
303 *uncovered*: bare-faced.

307 *proper saying*: likely story.

313 *count*: Beatrice makes a triple pun on 'count' (= Claudio, = account/narrative, = legal indictment).
Count Comfit: Count Candy.
316 *curtsies*: courtesies, ceremonies.
compliment: flattery.
317 *only . . . tongue*: become all talk.
trim: smooth.
318 *Hercules*: the superman of classical mythology.

Beatrice

Use it for my love some other way than swearing by it.

Benedick

Think you in your soul the Count Claudio hath wronged Hero?

Beatrice

325 Yea, as sure as I have a thought or a soul.

Benedick

Enough, I am engaged; I will challenge him. I will kiss your hand, and so I leave you. By this hand, Claudio shall render me a dear account. As you hear of me, so think of me. Go comfort your cousin. I

330 must say she is dead. And so, farewell.

[*Exeunt*

Act 4   Scene 2

Dogberry and Verges examine their prisoners.

0s.d. *gowns*: i.e. the official black gowns appropriate to their offices.

2 *stool . . . cushion*: i.e. so that he can sit and write notes.

5–6 *exhibition to examine*: commission to conduct an examination.

Scene 2

Enter Dogberry, Verges, *and the* Sexton *in gowns*; *and the* Watch, *with* Conrad *and* Borachio

Dogberry

Is our whole dissembly appeared?

Verges

O, a stool and a cushion for the sexton.

Sexton

[*Sits*] Which be the malefactors?

Dogberry

Marry, that am I, and my partner.

Verges

5 Nay, that's certain; we have the exhibition to examine.

Sexton

But which are the offenders that are to be examined? Let them come before Master Constable.

Dogberry

Yea, marry, let them come before me. What is your

10 name, friend?

Borachio

Borachio.

13 *sirrah*: A contemptuous form of 'sir', used to address social inferiors.

Dogberry

[*To the* Sexton] Pray write down 'Borachio'. [*To* Conrad] Yours, sirrah?

Conrad

I am a gentleman, sir, and my name is Conrad.

Dogberry

15 Write down 'Master Gentleman Conrad'. Masters, do you serve God?

Conrad and **Borachio**

Yea, sir, we hope.

Dogberry

Write down that they hope they serve God. And write 'God' first, for God defend but God should go

19 *defend*: forbid.

20 before such villains. Masters, it is proved already that you are little better than false knaves, and it will go near to be thought so shortly. How answer you for yourselves?

Conrad

Marry, sir, we say we are none.

Dogberry

25–6 *go about with*: get the better of.

25 A marvellous witty fellow, I assure you, but I will go about with him.—Come you hither, sirrah. A word in your ear, sir. I say to you it is thought you are false knaves.

Borachio

Sir, I say to you we are none.

Dogberry

30 Well, stand aside. Fore God, they are both in a tale. Have you writ down that they are none?

Sexton

Master Constable, you go not the way to examine. You must call forth the watch that are their accusers.

Dogberry

34 *eftest*: quickest.

Yea, marry, that's the eftest way. Let the watch come

35 forth.—Masters, I charge you in the prince's name accuse these men.

A Watchman

This man said, sir, that Don John, the prince's brother, was a villain.

Dogberry

Write down Prince John a villain. Why, this is flat

40 perjury, to call a prince's brother villain.

Borachio

Master Constable—

Dogberry

Pray thee, fellow, peace. I do not like thy look, I promise thee.

Sexton

What heard you him say else?

A Watchman

45 Marry, that he had received a thousand ducats of Don John for accusing the Lady Hero wrongfully.

Dogberry

Flat burglary, as ever was committed.

Verges

48 *by th' mass*: by the mass.

Yea, by th'mass, that it is.

Sexton

What else, fellow?

A Watchman

50 And that Count Claudio did mean upon his words to disgrace Hero before the whole assembly, and not marry her.

Dogberry

O villain! Thou wilt be condemned into everlasting redemption for this.

Sexton

55 What else?

A Watchman

This is all.

Sexton

And this is more, masters, than you can deny. Prince John is this morning secretly stolen away. Hero was in this manner accused, in this very manner refused, 60 and upon the grief of this suddenly died. Master Constable, let these men be bound and brought to Leonato's. I will go before and show him their examination.   [*Exit*

Dogberry

64 *opinioned*: pinioned, bound.

Come, let them be opinioned.

Verges

65 Let them be in the hands—

Watchmen *seize* Conrad *and* Borachio

66 *coxcomb*: fool (the fool's cap was
crowned with a crest like that of a cock).

67 *God s' my life*: May God save my life.
69 *naughty*: wicked.
73 *suspect*: i.e. 'respect'.

80 *pretty . . . flesh*: Dogberry is proud of his
appearance.
81 *go to*: 'I can tell you', 'believe me'; the
phrase is simply an intensifier.
82 *losses*: Even Dogberry's financial
disasters give him cause for self-
satisfaction.

Conrad
Off, coxcomb!

Dogberry
God s' my life, where's the sexton? Let him write
down the prince's officer coxcomb. Come, bind
them. [*To* Conrad, *who resists*]—Thou naughty
70 varlet!

Conrad
Away, you are an ass; you are an ass.

Dogberry
Dost thou not suspect my place? Dost thou not
suspect my years? O that he were here to write me
down an ass! But, masters, remember that I am an
75 ass. Though it be not written down, yet forget not
that I am an ass. No, thou villain, thou art full of
piety, as shall be proved upon thee by good witness.
I am a wise fellow, and which is more, an officer; and
which is more, a householder; and which is more, as
80 pretty a piece of flesh as any is in Messina; and one
that knows the law, go to; and a rich fellow enough,
go to; and a fellow that hath had losses; and one that
hath two gowns, and everything handsome about
him.—Bring him away. O that I had been writ down
85 an ass!   [*Exeunt*

Act 5

Act 5   Scene 1

Leonato, still grieving, attempts to challenge
Claudio. Don Pedro keeps the peace—but
Benedick presents a new challenge.
Dogberry brings in his prisoners, and
Borachio confesses all. Leonato promises a
new bride for Claudio.

2   *second*: assist.

7   *suit*: correspond.

12   *answer . . . strain*: respond with like
emotions (or musical tones).

16   *wag*: clear off.
      cry 'hem': clear his throat (before
      drinking).
17   *Patch*: mend, console.
      make . . . drunk: drown his sorrows.
18   *candle-wasters*: late-night drinkers.

22   *not feel*: do not feel.

24   *preceptial medicine*: proverbs as
      medicine.

27   *office*: business.

Scene 1

Enter Leonato *and* Antonio *his brother*

Antonio
If you go on thus, you will kill yourself,
And 'tis not wisdom thus to second grief
Against yourself.
Leonato
　　　　　　I pray thee cease thy counsel,
Which falls into mine ears as profitless
5 As water in a sieve. Give not me counsel,
Nor let no comforter delight mine ear
But such a one whose wrongs do suit with mine.
Bring me a father that so lov'd his child,
Whose joy of her is overwhelm'd like mine,
10 And bid him speak of patience.
Measure his woe the length and breadth of mine,
And let it answer every strain for strain,
As thus for thus, and such a grief for such,
In every lineament, branch, shape, and form.
15 If such a one will smile and stroke his beard,
Bid sorrow wag, cry 'hem' when he should groan,
Patch grief with proverbs, make misfortune drunk
With candle-wasters, bring him yet to me,
And I of him will gather patience.
20 But there is no such man. For, brother, men
Can counsel and speak comfort to that grief
Which they themselves not feel. But tasting it,
Their counsel turns to passion, which before
Would give preceptial medicine to rage,
25 Fetter strong madness in a silken thread,
Charm ache with air and agony with words.
No, no, 'tis all men's office to speak patience

To those that wring under the load of sorrow,
But no man's virtue nor sufficiency
30 To be so moral when he shall endure
The like himself. Therefore give me no counsel.
My griefs cry louder than advertisement.

Antonio
Therein do men from children nothing differ.

Leonato
I pray thee peace. I will be flesh and blood,
35 For there was never yet philosopher
That could endure the toothache patiently,
However they have writ the style of gods,
And made a pish at chance and sufferance.

Antonio
Yet bend not all the harm upon yourself.
40 Make those that do offend you suffer too.

Leonato
There thou speak'st reason; nay, I will do so.
My soul doth tell me Hero is belied,
And that shall Claudio know; so shall the prince,
And all of them that thus dishonour her.

Enter Don Pedro *the prince and* Claudio

Antonio
45 Here comes the prince and Claudio hastily.

Don Pedro
Good e'en, good e'en.

Claudio
                              Good day to both of you.

Leonato
Hear you, my lords!

Don Pedro
                              We have some haste, Leonato.

Leonato
Some haste, my lord! Well, fare you well, my lord.
Are you so hasty now? Well, all is one.

Don Pedro
50 Nay, do not quarrel with us, good old man.

Antonio
If he could right himself with quarrelling,
Some of us would lie low.

Claudio
                              Who wrongs him?

Leonato

Marry,

Thou dost wrong me, thou dissembler, thou.

Nay, never lay thy hand upon thy sword;

55 I fear thee not.

Claudio

Marry, beshrew my hand

If it should give your age such cause of fear.

In faith, my hand meant nothing to my sword.

Leonato

Tush, tush, man, never fleer and jest at me.

I speak not like a dotard nor a fool,

60 As under privilege of age to brag

What I have done being young, or what would do

Were I not old. Know, Claudio, to thy head,

Thou hast so wrong'd mine innocent child and me

That I am forc'd to lay my reverence by,

65 And with grey hairs and bruise of many days

Do challenge thee to trial of a man.

I say thou hast belied mine innocent child.

Thy slander hath gone through and through her heart,

And she lies buried with her ancestors—

70 O, in a tomb where never scandal slept

Save this of hers, fram'd by thy villainy.

Claudio

My villainy?

Leonato

Thine, Claudio, thine I say.

Don Pedro

You say not right, old man.

Leonato

My lord, my lord,

I'll prove it on his body if he dare,

75 Despite his nice fence and his active practice,

His May of youth and bloom of lustihood.

Claudio

Away, I will not have to do with you.

Leonato

Canst thou so doff me? Thou hast kill'd my child.

If thou kill'st me, boy, thou shalt kill a man.

---

53 *Thou*: The intimate form is intended as an insult.

55 *beshrew*: curse.

57 *meant nothing*: intended nothing (in moving toward the sword).

58 *fleer*: gibe.

62 *head*: face.
66 *trial of a man*: single combat.

71 *fram'd*: devised.
75 *nice fence*: fancy swordplay; Leonato scorns the elaborate new fencing techniques popular among the fashionable young men of Shakespeare's day.

78 *doff me*: put me off.
79 *boy*: Leonato uses the final insult.

82 *Win . . . me*: 'Let him overcome me,
and then he can boast' (proverbial).

84 *foining fence*: downward thrust in
fencing (here with sexual innuendo).

91 *apes*: mimics.
jacks: knaves.
94 *Scambling*: scuffling.
outfacing: insolent, bullying.
fashion-monging: constantly changing
fashions.

95 *cog and flout*: cheat and insult.
deprave: defame.
96 *Go anticly*: dress weirdly.
show . . . hideousness: look terrible.

Antonio
80 He shall kill two of us, and men indeed.
But that's no matter, let him kill one first.
Win me and wear me. Let him answer me.
Come follow me, boy; come, sir boy, come follow
me.
Sir boy, I'll whip you from your foining fence.
85 Nay, as I am a gentleman, I will.
Leonato
Brother—
Antonio
Content yourself. God knows, I lov'd my niece,
And she is dead, slander'd to death by villains
That dare as well answer a man in deed
90 As I dare take a serpent by the tongue.
Boys, apes, braggarts, jacks, milksops!
Leonato
                           Brother Antony—
Antonio
Hold you content. What, man, I know them, yea,
And what they weigh, even to the utmost scruple:
Scambling, outfacing, fashion-monging boys,
95 That lie and cog and flout, deprave and slander,
Go anticly, and show an outward hideousness,
And speak off half a dozen dangerous words,
How they might hurt their enemies, if they durst,
And this is all.
Leonato
100 But brother Antony—
Antonio
                      Come, 'tis no matter.
Do not you meddle, let me deal in this.
Don Pedro
Gentlemen both, we will not wake your patience.
My heart is sorry for your daughter's death,
But on my honour she was charg'd with nothing
105 But what was true and very full of proof.
Leonato
My lord, my lord—
Don Pedro
                 I will not hear you.

Leonato

No?

Come, brother, away. I will be heard.

Antonio

And shall, or some of us will smart for it.

[*Exeunt* Leonato *and* Antonio

Enter Benedick

Don Pedro

See, see, here comes the man we went to seek.

Claudio

110 Now, signor, what news?

Benedick

[*To* Don Pedro] Good day, my lord.

Don Pedro

Welcome, signor. You are almost come to part
almost a fray.

Claudio

We had liked to have had our two noses snapped off

115 with two old men without teeth.

Don Pedro

Leonato and his brother. What thinkest thou? Had
we fought, I doubt we should have been too young
for them.

Benedick

In a false quarrel there is no true valour. I came to

120 seek you both.

Claudio

We have been up and down to seek thee, for we are
high-proof melancholy and would fain have it beaten
away. Wilt thou use thy wit?

Benedick

It is in my scabbard. Shall I draw it?

Don Pedro

125 Dost thou wear thy wit by thy side?

Claudio

Never any did so, though very many have been
beside their wit. I will bid thee draw as we do the
minstrels; draw to pleasure us.

Don Pedro

As I am an honest man, he looks pale. Art thou sick,

130 or angry?

114 *had liked*: were likely.
115 *with*: by.

117 *doubt*: fear.

122 *high-proof*: in the highest degree of.

131 *care . . . cat*: A proverbial warning
     against too much worry.

133 *in the career*: in mid-gallop (as in
     jousting).
     an: if.

135 *staff*: lance.
135–6 *broke cross*: snapped across the middle
     (because not aimed for a direct strike
     against the opponent).

139 *turn his girdle*: what he can do about it;
     the expression is proverbial.

143 *make it good*: back up what I say.
144 *Do me right*: accept my challenge.
     protest: proclaim.

147–8 *so . . . cheer*: so long as I am well
     entertained.

150 *calf's head*: fool.
151 *capon*: coward (a castrated cockerel).
152 *curiously*: skilfully.
     naught: rubbish.
153 *woodcock*: idiot (the bird was proverbially
     gullible).
154 *ambles well*: goes along very slowly.

155 *wit*: understanding—but the sense
     probably develops with sexual innuendo.

Claudio

What, courage, man! What though care killed a cat,
thou hast mettle enough in thee to kill care.

Benedick

Sir, I shall meet your wit in the career, an you charge
it against me. I pray you choose another subject.

Claudio

135 Nay then, give him another staff. This last was broke
cross.

Don Pedro

By this light, he changes more and more. I think he
be angry indeed.

Claudio

If he be, he knows how to turn his girdle.

Benedick

140 Shall I speak a word in your ear?

Claudio

God bless me from a challenge.

Benedick

[*Aside to* Claudio] You are a villain. I jest not. I will
make it good how you dare, with what you dare, and
when you dare. Do me right, or I will protest your
145 cowardice. You have killed a sweet lady, and her
death shall fall heavy on you. Let me hear from you.

Claudio

[*Aside to* Benedick] Well, I will meet you, so I may
have good cheer.

Don Pedro

What, a feast, a feast?

Claudio

150 I' faith, I thank him. He hath bid me to a calf's head
and a capon, the which if I do not carve most
curiously, say my knife's naught. Shall I not find a
woodcock too?

Benedick

Sir, your wit ambles well; it goes easily.

Don Pedro

155 I'll tell thee how Beatrice praised thy wit the other
day. I said thou hadst a fine wit. 'True,' said she, 'a
fine little one.' 'No,' said I, 'a great wit.' 'Right,' says
she, 'a great gross one.' 'Nay,' said I, 'a good wit.'
'Just,' said she, 'it hurts nobody.' 'Nay,' said I, 'the

161 *hath the tongues*: speaks foreign languages.

167 *properest*: finest, most handsome.

170 *an if*: if indeed.

172 *daughter*: Don Pedro (or perhaps the dramatist) has forgotten that Hero is dead.

173–4 *God . . . garden*: Adam was trying, unsuccessfully, to hide himself from God (Genesis 3:8).

175–6 *savage . . . head*: Don Pedro seems unaware that the happy jokes of *Act 1, Scene 1* are no longer appropriate.

180 *gossip-like humour*: chattering like old women (gossips = godparents).

160 gentleman is wise.' 'Certain,' said she, 'a wise gentleman.' 'Nay,' said I, 'he hath the tongues.' 'That I believe,' said she, 'for he swore a thing to me on Monday night which he forswore on Tuesday morning. There's a double tongue; there's two

165 tongues.' Thus did she an hour together trans-shape thy particular virtues. Yet at last she concluded with a sigh thou wast the properest man in Italy.

Claudio
For the which she wept heartily and said she cared not.

Don Pedro
170 Yea, that she did. But yet for all that, an if she did not hate him deadly, she would love him dearly. The old man's daughter told us all.

Claudio
All, all. And moreover, God saw him when he was hid in the garden.

Don Pedro
175 But when shall we set the savage bull's horns on the sensible Benedick's head?

Claudio
Yea, and text underneath, 'Here dwells Benedick the married man'.

Benedick
[*To* Claudio] Fare you well, boy, you know my mind.
180 I will leave you now to your gossip-like humour. You break jests as braggarts do their blades which, God be thanked, hurt not. [*To* Don Pedro] My lord, for your many courtesies I thank you. I must discontinue your company. Your brother the bastard
185 is fled from Messina. You have among you killed a sweet and innocent lady. For my Lord Lackbeard there, he and I shall meet; and till then, peace be with him.   [*Exit*

Don Pedro
He is in earnest.

Claudio
190 In most profound earnest and, I'll warrant you, for the love of Beatrice.

Don Pedro
And hath challenged thee?

Claudio
Most sincerely.

Don Pedro
What a pretty thing man is when he goes in his
195 doublet and hose and leaves off his wit!

Enter Dogberry *and* Verges, *the* Watch,
Conrad, *and* Borachio

Claudio
He is then a giant to an ape. But then is an ape a
doctor to such a man.

Don Pedro
But soft you, let me be. Pluck up, my heart, and be
sad. Did he not say my brother was fled?

Dogberry
200 [*To a* prisoner] Come you, sir. If justice cannot tame
you, she shall ne'er weigh more reasons in her
balance. Nay, an you be a cursing hypocrite once,
you must be looked to.

Don Pedro
How now, two of my brother's men bound? Borachio
205 one!

Claudio
Hearken after their offence, my lord.

Don Pedro
Officers, what offence have these men done?

Dogberry
Marry, sir, they have committed false report.
Moreover they have spoken untruths; secondarily
210 they are slanders; sixth and lastly they have belied a
lady; thirdly they have verified unjust things and, to
conclude, they are lying knaves.

Don Pedro
First I ask thee what they have done; thirdly I ask
thee what's their offence; sixth and lastly why they
215 are committed and, to conclude, what you lay to
their charge.

Claudio
Rightly reasoned and in his own division. And by my
troth there's one meaning well suited.

Don Pedro
[*To* Conrad *and* Borachio] Who have you offended,
220 masters, that you are thus bound to your answer?

---

194 *goes*: goes out wearing.

196–7 *He is . . . man*: a fool may then think
such a man a hero, but then, compared
to such a man, a fool is a scholar.
197 *doctor*: learned man, scholar.
198–9 *Pluck . . . sad*: pull yourself together
and be serious.

201 *reasons*: The word was pronounced
'raisins'—allowing Dogberry an easy
pun.
202 *cursing*: accursed.
206 *Hearken after*: enquire about.

217 *in . . . division*: with the argument
properly set out.
218 *one . . . suited*: Between them, Dogberry
and Don Pedro have presented one idea
in six ways.

This learned constable is too cunning to be understood. What's your offence?

Borachio

Sweet Prince, let me go no farther to mine answer. Do you hear me, and let this count kill me. I have deceived even your very eyes. What your wisdoms could not discover, these shallow fools have brought to light, who in the night overheard me confessing to this man how Don John your brother incensed me to slander the Lady Hero, how you were brought into the orchard and saw me court Margaret in Hero's garments, how you disgraced her when you should marry her. My villainy they have upon record, which I had rather seal with my death than repeat over to my shame. The lady is dead upon mine and my master's false accusation; and, briefly, I desire nothing but the reward of a villain.

Don Pedro

[*To* Claudio] Runs not this speech like iron through your blood?

Claudio

I have drunk poison whiles he uttered it.

Don Pedro

[*To* Borachio] But did my brother set thee on to this?

Borachio

Yea, and paid me richly for the practice of it.

Don Pedro

He is compos'd and fram'd of treachery,
And fled he is upon this villainy.

Claudio

Sweet Hero, now thy image doth appear
In the rare semblance that I lov'd it first.

Dogberry

Come, bring away the plaintiffs. By this time our sexton hath reformed Signor Leonato of the matter. And, masters, do not forget to specify, when time and place shall serve, that I am an ass.

Verges

Here, here comes Master Signor Leonato, and the sexton too.

230–1 *in Hero's garments*: This detail has not been mentioned before.

241 *practice*: performance.

245 *rare semblance*: wonderful likeness.

Enter Leonato, Antonio *his brother, and the*
Sexton

Leonato
Which is the villain? Let me see his eyes,
That when I note another man like him
I may avoid him. Which of these is he?
Borachio
255 If you would know your wronger, look on me.
Leonato
Art thou the slave that with thy breath hast kill'd
Mine innocent child?
Borachio
                                    Yea, even I alone.
Leonato
No, not so, villain, thou beliest thyself.
Here stand a pair of honourable men.
260 A third is fled that had a hand in it.
I thank you, princes, for my daughter's death.
Record it with your high and worthy deeds.
'Twas bravely done, if you bethink you of it.
Claudio
I know not how to pray your patience,
265 Yet I must speak. Choose your revenge yourself;
Impose me to what penance your invention
Can lay upon my sin. Yet sinn'd I not
But in mistaking.
Don Pedro
                                    By my soul, nor I.
And yet to satisfy this good old man
270 I would bend under any heavy weight
That he'll enjoin me to.
Leonato
I cannot bid you bid my daughter live;
That were impossible; but, I pray you both,
Possess the people in Messina here
275 How innocent she died. And if your love
Can labour aught in sad invention,
Hang her an epitaph upon her tomb
And sing it to her bones; sing it tonight.
Tomorrow morning come you to my house,
280 And since you could not be my son-in-law,
Be yet my nephew. My brother hath a daughter,

264 *patience*: The word must be pronounced with three syllables.

266 *Impose me*: impose on me.
invention: The word here has only three syllables (unlike the pronunciation at line 276).

274 *Possess*: inform.

276 *invention*: imagination; the word here has four syllables.
277–8 *Hang . . . tonight*: i.e. as suggested by the friar, *4, 1, 205–7*.

283 *heir . . . us*: Antonio's son (*1*, *2*, *1*) has been forgotten—and the daughter is an invention of the moment.

284 *right*: legal right *and* marriage rite.

290 *naughty*: wicked (the sense was stronger than it is today).

292 *pack'd*: involved as an accomplice.

298 *under . . . black*: written down.

301 *one Deformed*: 'what a deformed thief this fashion is' (*3*, *3*, 115).

302 *a key . . . lock*: 'a wears a lock' (*3*, *3*, 157–8); Dogberry elaborates the lovelock.

303 *in God's name*: a phrase commonly used by beggars: 'He that hath pity upon the poor lendeth unto the Lord' (Proverbs 19:17).
     used: been in the habit of doing.

311 *God . . . foundation*: a phrase used by institutional beggars.

Almost the copy of my child that's dead,
And she alone is heir to both of us.
Give her the right you should have giv'n her cousin,
285 And so dies my revenge.

Claudio
                              O noble sir!
Your overkindness doth wring tears from me.
I do embrace your offer, and dispose
For henceforth of poor Claudio.

Leonato
Tomorrow then I will expect your coming;
290 Tonight I take my leave. This naughty man
Shall face to face be brought to Margaret,
Who, I believe, was pack'd in all this wrong,
Hir'd to it by your brother.

Borachio
                              No, by my soul, she was not;
Nor knew not what she did when she spoke to me,
295 But always hath been just and virtuous
In anything that I do know by her.

Dogberry
[*To* Leonato] Moreover, sir, which indeed is not under white and black, this plaintiff here, the offender, did call me ass. I beseech you let it be
300 remembered in his punishment. And also the watch heard them talk of one Deformed. They say he wears a key in his ear and lock hanging by it, and borrows money in God's name, the which he hath used so long and never paid, that now men grow hard-
305 hearted and will lend nothing for God's sake. Pray you examine him upon that point.

Leonato
I thank thee for thy care and honest pains.

Dogberry
Your worship speaks like a most thankful and reverend youth, and I praise God for you.

Leonato
310 [*Giving him money*] There's for thy pains.

Dogberry
God save the foundation!

Leonato
Go, I discharge thee of thy prisoner, and I thank thee.

Dogberry

315 I leave an arrant knave with your worship, which I beseech your worship to correct yourself, for the example of others. God keep your worship; I wish your worship well. God restore you to health. I humbly give you leave to depart, and if a merry meeting may be wished, God prohibit it. Come,
320 neighbour.   [*Exeunt* Dogberry *and* Verges

Leonato

Until tomorrow morning, lords, farewell.

Antonio

Farewell, my lords. We look for you tomorrow.

Don Pedro

We will not fail.

Claudio

               Tonight I'll mourn with Hero.

                  [*Exeunt* Don Pedro *and* Claudio

Leonato

[*To the* Watch] Bring you these fellows on.—We'll talk with Margaret,

325 How her acquaintance grew with this lewd fellow.

                         [*Exeunt*

325 *lewd*: base.

Act 5   Scene 2

Benedick tries to write a poem for Beatrice.

5 *so high a style*: Benedick puns on style (= literary manner) and stile (= steps or rungs for climbing over a fence); the 'high style' of literature was used only for works of great seriousness.

6 *come over*: surpass, get across: Margaret is quick to hear sexual innuendo.

9 *keep below stairs*: i.e. remain a servant (and not become a mistress).

Scene 2

Enter Benedick *and* Margaret

Benedick

Pray thee, sweet Mistress Margaret, deserve well at my hands by helping me to the speech of Beatrice.

Margaret

Will you then write me a sonnet in praise of my beauty?

Benedick

5 In so high a style, Margaret, that no man living shall come over it, for in most comely truth, thou deservest it.

Margaret

To have no man come over me? Why, shall I always keep below stairs?

11   *catches*: picks things up quickly.
15–16   *give . . . bucklers*: throw down my
defences ('bucklers' = small shields.

18–19   *put in . . . vice*: use a screw to fit the
pikes (into the bucklers).

24–7   *The god . . . deserve*: Benedick sings a
popular song—see 'Benedick's Song',
p.103.

28   *Leander*: In Greek mythology, Leander
swam every night across the Hellespont
that separated him from his beloved
Hero; the story is told in Christopher
Marlowe's poem *Hero and Leander*
(published 1598), which may have
suggested the name for Shakespeare's
character.
29   *Troilus*: In the Trojan War, Troilus was
introduced to Cressida by her uncle,
Pandarus; and their story is the subject
of Shakespeare's play *Troilus and
Cressida*.
30   *quondam carpet-mongers*: old-time ladies'
men (who frequented carpeted
boudoirs).
31   *yet*: still.
35   *innocent*: simple enough.
39   *festival terms*: flowery language.

Benedick

10 Thy wit is as quick as the greyhound's mouth; it
catches.

Margaret

And yours as blunt as the fencer's foils, which hit but
hurt not.

Benedick

A most manly wit, Margaret; it will not hurt a
15 woman. And so, I pray thee, call Beatrice. I give thee
the bucklers.

Margaret

Give us the swords; we have bucklers of our own.

Benedick

If you use them, Margaret, you must put in the pikes
with a vice; and they are dangerous weapons for
20 maids.

Margaret

Well, I will call Beatrice to you, who I think hath
legs.   [*Exit*

Benedick

And therefore will come.
[*Sings*]
        The god of love
25   That sits above,
        And knows me, and knows me,
        How pitiful I deserve—

I mean in singing. But in loving—Leander the good
swimmer, Troilus the first employer of panders, and
30 a whole book full of these quondam carpet-mongers
whose names yet run smoothly in the even road of a
blank verse—why they were never so truly turned
over and over as my poor self in love. Marry, I
cannot show it in rhyme. I have tried. I can find out
35 no rhyme to 'lady' but 'baby'—an innocent rhyme;
for 'scorn' 'horn'—a hard rhyme; for 'school'
'fool'—a babbling rhyme. Very ominous endings.
No, I was not born under a rhyming planet, nor I
cannot woo in festival terms.

Enter Beatrice

40 Sweet Beatrice, wouldst thou come when I called thee?

Beatrice

Yea, signor, and depart when you bid me.

Benedick

O, stay but till then.

Beatrice

'Then' is spoken. Fare you well now. And yet, ere I
45 go, let me go with that I came for, which is with knowing what hath passed between you and Claudio.

Benedick

Only foul words, and thereupon I will kiss thee.

Beatrice

Foul words is but foul wind, and foul wind is but foul breath, and foul breath is noisome. Therefore I will
50 depart unkissed.

Benedick

Thou hast frighted the word out of his right sense, so forcible is thy wit. But I must tell thee plainly, Claudio undergoes my challenge; and either I must shortly hear from him or I will subscribe him a
55 coward. And I pray thee now tell me, for which of my bad parts didst thou first fall in love with me?

Beatrice

For them all together, which maintained so politic a state of evil that they will not admit any good part to intermingle with them. But for which of my good
60 parts did you first suffer love for me?

Benedick

'Suffer love'—a good epithet. I do suffer love indeed, for I love thee against my will.

Beatrice

In spite of your heart, I think. Alas, poor heart! If you spite it for my sake I will spite it for yours, for I
65 will never love that which my friend hates.

Benedick

Thou and I are too wise to woo peaceably.

Beatrice

It appears not in this confession. There's not one wise man among twenty that will praise himself.

49 *is noisome*: stinks.

54 *subscribe him*: make a signed statement that he is.

57–8 *so . . . state*: such a well-organized rule.

61 *epithet*: expression.

64 *spite it*: vex, irritate it.

67 *appears not*: doesn't seem so.

69 *instance*: argument.
70 *good neighbours*: Benedick alludes to a proverb: 'He who praises himself has ill neighbours'.
72 *in monument*: in remembrance.

75 *Question*: good question—and Benedick provides the answer.
76 *rheum*: tears.
77 *Don Worm*: The worm, gnawing inwardly, is a traditional image for the conscience (Isaiah 66:24, Mark 9:44).

87–8 *old coil*: great confusion, much ado.

90 *abused*: deceived.
91 *presently*: immediately.

93 *die*: Benedick's romanticism includes the word's sexual sense (= orgasm).

Benedick
An old, an old instance, Beatrice, that lived in the
70 time of good neighbours. If a man do not erect in
this age his own tomb ere he dies, he shall live no
longer in monument than the bell rings and the
widow weeps.
Beatrice
And how long is that, think you?
Benedick
75 Question—why, an hour in clamour and a quarter in
rheum. Therefore is it most expedient for the wise, if
Don Worm his conscience find no impediment to
the contrary, to be the trumpet of his own virtues, as
I am to myself. So much for praising myself who—I
80 myself will bear witness—is praiseworthy. And now
tell me, how doth your cousin?
Beatrice
Very ill.
Benedick
And how do you?
Beatrice
Very ill too.
Benedick
85 Serve God, love me, and mend. There will I leave
you too, for here comes one in haste.

Enter Ursula

Ursula
Madam, you must come to your uncle. Yonder's old
coil at home. It is proved my Lady Hero hath been
falsely accused, the prince and Claudio mightily
90 abused, and Don John is the author of all, who is fled
and gone. Will you come presently?
Beatrice
Will you go hear this news, signor?
Benedick
I will live in thy heart, die in thy lap, and be buried
in thy eyes; and, moreover, I will go with thee to thy
95 uncle's.   [*Exeunt*

Act 5   Scene 3

Claudio performs his duties at Hero's tomb.

os.d. *tapers*: wax candles for devotional
use.

5 *guerdon of*: recompense for.

Scene 3

> *Enter* Claudio, Don Pedro *the prince, and
> three or four* Attendants *with tapers, all
> wearing mourning*; Balthasar *and*
> musicians

Claudio
Is this the monument of Leonato?
A Lord
It is, my lord.
Claudio
[*Reading from a scroll*]
  Done to death by slanderous tongues
    Was the Hero that here lies.
5   Death, in guerdon of her wrongs,
    Gives her fame which never dies.
  So the life that died with shame
  Lives in death with glorious fame.

> *He hangs the epitaph on the tomb*

  Hang thou there upon the tomb,
10   Praising her when I am dumb.
  Now music sound, and sing your solemn hymn.

> *Musicians play*

11 **Balthasar**: The singer of *Act 2,
Scene 3.* No singer is named in the
Quarto text, although lines 12–21 are
marked 'Song'.

12 *goddess of the night*: Diana, the moon-
goddess, protector of virgins (her
'knights').

15 *Round . . . go*: The mourners circle the
tomb clockwise in a propitiatory dance.

20 *uttered*: utterèd; expressed, set forth; the
rhyme here is more important than the
sense.

24–33 *Good morrow . . . woe*: The rhyming
lines declare the closure of an episode.

26 *wheels of Phoebus*: chariot of the sun-god.

29 *several*: separate.

30 *weeds*: garments.

32 *Hymen*: god of marriage.
luckier issue: more fortunate outcome.
speeds: hastens.

Balthasar

[*Sings*]
   Pardon, goddess of the night,
   Those that slew thy virgin knight,
   For the which with songs of woe
15   Round about her tomb they go.
      Midnight, assist our moan,
      Help us to sigh and groan,
         Heavily, heavily.
   Graves yawn, and yield your dead
20   Till death be uttered,
         Heavily, heavily.

   Claudio
   Now, unto thy bones good night.
   Yearly will I do this rite.

   Don Pedro
   Good morrow, masters, put your torches out.
25   The wolves have prey'd, and look, the gentle day
   Before the wheels of Phoebus round about
      Dapples the drowsy east with spots of grey.
   Thanks to you all, and leave us. Fare you well.

   Claudio
   Good morrow, masters. Each his several way.

   Don Pedro
30 Come, let us hence, and put on other weeds,
   And then to Leonato's we will go.

   Claudio
   And Hymen now with luckier issue speeds
   Than this for whom we render'd up this woe.

                                      [*Exeunt*

Act 5   Scene 4

Claudio, prepared to meet his new bride, is reunited with Hero, then Benedick joins hands with Beatrice and leads the company off into a final dance.

6 *question*: investigation.

7 *sorts*: turns out.

8 *faith*: honour.

14 *office*: function.

17 *confirm'd countenance*: a straight face; 'confirm'd' must be stressed on the first syllable.

20 *undo me*: ruin me, release me (from the pose of misogynist).

Scene 4

Enter Leonato, Antonio, Benedick, Beatrice, Margaret, Ursula, Friar Francis, *and* Hero

Friar
Did I not tell you she was innocent?
Leonato
So are the prince and Claudio, who accus'd her
Upon the error that you heard debated.
But Margaret was in some fault for this,
5 Although against her will, as it appears
In the true course of the question.
Antonio
Well, I am glad that all things sorts so well.
Benedick
And so am I, being else by faith enforc'd
To call young Claudio to a reckoning for it.
Leonato
10 Well, daughter, and you gentlewomen all,
Withdraw into a chamber by yourselves,
And when I send for you, come hither mask'd.
    [*Exeunt* Beatrice, Hero, Margaret, *and* Ursula
The prince and Claudio promis'd by this hour
To visit me. [*To* Antonio] You know your office, brother;
15 You must be father to your brother's daughter,
And give her to young Claudio.
Antonio
Which I will do with confirm'd countenance.
Benedick
Friar, I must entreat your pains, I think.
Friar
To do what, signor?
Benedick
20 To bind me or undo me, one of them.
Signor Leonato, truth it is, good signor,
Your niece regards me with an eye of favour.
Leonato
That eye my daughter lent her, 'tis most true.
Benedick
And I do with an eye of love requite her.

Leonato

25 The sight whereof I think you had from me,
From Claudio and the prince. But what's your will?

Benedick

Your answer, sir, is enigmatical.
But for my will—my will is your good will
May stand with ours this day to be conjoin'd

30 In the state of honourable marriage—
In which, good friar, I shall desire your help.

Leonato

My heart is with your liking.

Friar

And my help.
Here comes the prince and Claudio.

Enter Don Pedro *and* Claudio *with*
Attendants

Don Pedro

Good morrow to this fair assembly.

Leonato

35 Good morrow, Prince. Good morrow, Claudio.
We here attend you. Are you yet determin'd
Today to marry with my brother's daughter?

Claudio

I'll hold my mind, were she an Ethiope.

Leonato

Call her forth, brother; here's the friar ready.

[*Exit* Antonio

Don Pedro

40 Good morrow, Benedick. Why, what's the matter
That you have such a February face,
So full of frost, of storm and cloudiness?

Claudio

I think he thinks upon the savage bull.
Tush, fear not, man, we'll tip thy horns with gold,

45 And all Europa shall rejoice at thee
As once Europa did at lusty Jove
When he would play the noble beast in love.

Benedick

Bull Jove, sir, had an amiable low,
And some such strange bull leapt your father's cow

50 And got a calf in that same noble feat
Much like to you, for you have just his bleat.

30 *marriage*: The word must be
pronounced with three syllables.

34 *assembly*: This word needs four syllables
for regularity.

38 *Ethiope*: Ethiopian—i.e. very dark
(suntan was most unfashionable at this
time).

41 *February face*: Benedick still shows his
disapproval of Don Pedro and Claudio.

43–7 *savage bull . . . love*: Classical
mythology tells how Jupiter (Jove)
transformed himself into a bull and
carried off the princess Europa.

44 *tip . . . gold*: make you a glorious
cuckold.

45 *all Europa*: i.e. the entire continent of
Europe.

46 *once Europa did*: i.e. the princess Europa.

Enter Antonio *with* Hero, Beatrice,
Margaret, *and* Ursula, *the ladies masked*

Claudio

For this I owe you. Here comes other reck'nings.
Which is the lady I must seize upon?

Antonio

This same is she, and I do give you her.

Claudio

55 Why then, she's mine. Sweet, let me see your face.

Leonato

No, that you shall not till you take her hand
Before this friar and swear to marry her.

Claudio

[*To* Hero] Give me your hand before this holy friar.
I am your husband, if you like of me.

Hero

60 [*Unmasking*] And when I liv'd I was your other wife;
And when you lov'd, you were my other husband.

Claudio

Another Hero!

Hero

                        Nothing certainer.
One Hero died defil'd, but I do live,
And surely as I live, I am a maid.

Don Pedro

65 The former Hero, Hero that is dead!

Leonato

She died, my lord, but whiles her slander liv'd.

Friar

All this amazement can I qualify.
When after that the holy rites are ended
I'll tell you largely of fair Hero's death.

70 Meantime let wonder seem familiar,
And to the chapel let us presently.

Benedick

Soft and fair, friar; which is Beatrice?

Beatrice

[*Unmasking*] I answer to that name. What is your
will?

Benedick

Do not you love me?

67   *qualify*: moderate.

69   *largely*: fully.

71   *presently*: at once.

72   *Soft and fair*: take it easy.

Beatrice

Why no, no more than reason.

Benedick

75 Why then, your uncle and the prince and Claudio
Have been deceiv'd. They swore you did.

Beatrice

Do not you love me?

Benedick

Troth no, no more than reason.

Beatrice

Why then, my cousin, Margaret, and Ursula
Are much deceiv'd, for they did swear you did.

Benedick

80 They swore that you were almost sick for me.

Beatrice

They swore that you were well nigh dead for me.

Benedick

'Tis no such matter. Then you do not love me?

Beatrice

No, truly, but in friendly recompense.

Leonato

Come, cousin, I am sure you love the gentleman.

Claudio

85 And I'll be sworn upon't that he loves her,
For here's a paper written in his hand,
A halting sonnet of his own pure brain,
Fashion'd to Beatrice.

Hero

And here's another,
Writ in my cousin's hand, stol'n from her pocket,
90 Containing her affection unto Benedick.

Benedick

A miracle! Here's our own hands against our hearts.
Come, I will have thee. But by this light, I take thee
for pity.

Beatrice

I would not deny you. But by this good day, I yield
95 upon great persuasion, and partly to save your life,
for I was told you were in a consumption.

Benedick

[*Kissing her*] Peace, I will stop your mouth.

Don Pedro

How dost thou, 'Benedick the married man'?

83 *but in . . . recompense*: except as a return of friendship.

87 *halting*: metrically lame.

Benedick

I'll tell thee what, Prince: a college of wit-crackers
100 cannot flout me out of my humour. Dost thou think
I care for a satire or an epigram? No, if a man will be
beaten with brains, a shall wear nothing handsome
about him. In brief, since I do purpose to marry, I
will think nothing to any purpose that the world can
105 say against it. And therefore never flout at me for
what I have said against it. For man is a giddy thing,
and this is my conclusion. For thy part, Claudio, I
did think to have beaten thee, but in that thou art
like to be my kinsman, live unbruised, and love my
110 cousin.

Claudio

I had well hoped thou wouldst have denied Beatrice,
that I might have cudgelled thee out of thy single life
to make thee a double dealer, which out of question
thou wilt be, if my cousin do not look exceeding
115 narrowly to thee.

Benedick

Come, come, we are friends. Let's have a dance ere
we are married, that we may lighten our own hearts
and our wives' heels.

Leonato

We'll have dancing afterward.

Benedick

120 First, of my word! Therefore play, music. [*To* Don
Pedro] Prince, thou art sad. Get thee a wife, get thee
a wife. There is no staff more reverend than one
tipped with horn.

Enter Messenger

Messenger

My lord, your brother John is ta'en in flight,
125 And brought with armed men back to Messina.

Benedick

Think not on him till tomorrow. I'll devise thee brave
punishments for him. Strike up, pipers.

[*Dance, and exeunt*

101 *satire . . . epigram*: These forms of
ridicule were popular at the time.
102 *wear nothing handsome*: not wear
fashionable clothes (which were an easy
and popular target for satirists).
105 *flout*: mock.
106 *giddy*: inconstant.

113 *double dealer*: i.e. an unfaithful husband.

122–3 *There . . . horn*: The play's final
allusion to the horns of the cuckold; the
'staff' is 'reverend' because it is a
symbol of authority, and old age.
126 *brave*: fine.

Benedick's Song

High on the charts in the sixteenth century was the song that Benedick attempts to sing when he is waiting for Beatrice in *Act 5, Scene 2*. Its author was William Elderton, actor, singer, and songwriter, who died *c.* 1592, and the song's popularity is vouched for by the number of imitations, parodies, and references in the literature of the period. It was set to a well-known dance tune called 'Turkeyloney'.

1   The gods of love that sits about
        and know me, and know me,
              how sorrowful I do serve,
  grant my request that at the least,
        she show me, she show me,
            some pity when I deserve;
that every brawl may turn to bliss,
      to joy with all that joyful is.
          Do this my dear and bind me
  for ever and ever your own;
      And as you here do find me
         so let your love be shown,
  for till I hear this unity
    I languish in extremity.

2   As yet I have a soul to save
        uprightly, uprightly;
           though troubled with despair,
  I cannot find to set my mind
        so lightly, so slightly,
           as die before you be there.
But since I must needs you provoke,
      come slake the thirst, stand by the stroke,
that when my heart is fainted
      the sorrowful sighs may tell
you might have been acquainted
      with one that loved you well.
None have I told the jeopardy
      that none but you can remedy . . .

5   With courtesy now so bend, so bow,
          to speed me, to speed me,
               as answereth my desire;
as I will be if ever I see
       you need, you need me,
            as ready when you require.
Unworthy though to come so nigh
       that passing show that feeds mine eye,
yet shall I die without it
       if pity be not in you.
            But sure I do not doubt it
nor anything you can do—
to whom I do commit, and shall,
       my self to work your will with all.

finis

'A Hero-ic puzzle'

The author of *Alice in Wonderland*, Lewis Carroll, was quick to appreciate the many improbabilities of the situations in *Much Ado About Nothing*, and he amused himself by pointing out some of them to Ellen Terry, a famous actress of the time.

Christ Church
Oxford
20 March 1883

Dear Mrs Wardell [Ellen Terry's married name],

I'm going to put before you a 'Hero-ic' puzzle of mine—

Why in the world did not Hero (or at any rate Beatrice speaking on her behalf) prove an 'alibi', in answer to the charge? It seems certain she did *not* sleep in her own room that night: for how could Margaret venture to open the window and talk from it, with her mistress asleep in the room? It would be sure to wake her. Besides, Borachio says, after promising that Margaret shall speak with him out of Hero's chamber-window, 'I will so fashion the matter that Hero shall be absent'. (How *he* could possibly manage any such thing is another difficulty: but I pass over that.)

Well then, granting that Hero slept in some other room that night why didn't she say so? When Claudio asks her, 'What man was he talked with you yesternight Out at your window betwixt twelve and one?' why doesn't she reply, 'I talked with no man at that hour, my lord: Nor was I in my chamber yesternight, But in another, far from it remote'. And this she could of course prove by the evidence of the housemaid, who *must* have known that she had occupied another room that night.

But even if *Hero* might be supposed to be so distracted as not to remember where she had slept the night before, or even whether she had slept *anywhere*, surely *Beatrice* has her wits about her? And when an arrangement was made, by which she was to lose, for that one night, her twelve-months' bedfellow, is it conceivable that she didn't know *where* Hero passed the night? Why didn't she reply

> But, good my lord, sweet Hero slept not there:
> She had another chamber for the nonce.
> 'Twas sure some counterfeit that did present
> Her person at the window, aped her voice,

Her mien, her manners, and hath thus deceived
My good lord Pedro and this company?

With all these excellent materials for proving an 'alibi', it is incomprehensible that no one should think of it. If only there had been a barrister present, to cross-examine Beatrice! 'Now, ma'am, attend to me, if you please: and speak up, so that the jury may hear you. Where did you sleep last night? Where did Hero sleep? Will you swear that she slept in her own room? Will you swear you do not know where she slept? Etc, etc' . . .

C. L. Dodgson (Lewis Carroll)

From *The Letters of Lewis Carroll*, ed. Morton N. Cohen (1979), i. 488.

Classwork and Examinations

The plays of Shakespeare are studied all over the world, and this classroom edition is being used in many different countries. Teaching methods vary from school to school and there are many different ways of examining a student's work. Some teachers and examiners expect detailed knowledge of Shakespeare's text; others ask for imaginative involvement with his characters and their situations; and there are some teachers who want their students, by means of 'workshop' activities, to share in the theatrical experience of directing and performing a play. Most people use a variety of methods, and this section of the book offers a few suggestions for approaches to *Much Ado About Nothing* which could be used in schools and colleges to help with students' understanding and *enjoyment* of the play.

> A Discussion
> B Character Study
> C Activities
> D Context Questions
> E Comprehension and Appreciation Questions
> F Essays
> G Projects

A Discussion

Talking about the play—about the issues it raises and the characters who are involved—is one of the most rewarding and pleasurable ways of studying Shakespeare. It makes sense to discuss each scene as it is read, sharing impressions—and perhaps correcting misapprehensions. It can be useful to compare aspects of this play with other fictions—plays, novels, films—or with modern life. A large class can divide into small groups, each with a leader, who can discuss different aspects of a single topic and then report back to the main assembly.

Suggestions

A1 What makes you laugh? Are there different kinds of laughter? Do you laugh at the same things as your parents?

A2   'By my troth, niece, thou wilt never get thee a husband if thou be so shrewd of thy tongue' (2, 1, 16–17). Is it true that men don't like/are afraid of clever women?

A3   'Well, niece, I trust you will be ruled by your father'. 'It is my cousin's duty to make curtsy and say, "Father, as it please you"' (2, 1, 44–7). How much should parents influence their children's choice of marriage-partners?

A4   'Friendship is constant in all other things Save in the office and affairs of love' (2, 1, 163–4). Which matters most to you—love or friendship?

A5   'I would fain have it a match' (2, 1, 339). Have you ever tried match-making among your friends? What do you see as the dangers here?

A6   'till all graces be in one woman, one woman shall not come in my grace. Rich she shall be, that's certain. Wise, or I'll none. Virtuous, or I'll never cheapen her . . . ' (2, 3, 28–31). What are your specifications for a marriage-partner? Would you settle for less?

A7   Would you stage this play in anything other than Elizabethan dress? What might be gained—or lost—by this?

B   Character Study

Shakespeare is famous for his creation of characters who seem like real people. We can judge their actions and we can try to comprehend their thoughts and feelings—just as we criticize and try to understand the people we know. As the play progresses, we learn to like or dislike, love or hate, them—just as though they lived in *our* world.

Characters can be studied *from the outside*, by observing what they do and listening sensitively to what they say. This is the scholar's method: the scholar—or any reader—has access to the entire play, and can see the function of every character within the whole scheme of that play.

Another approach works *from the inside*, taking a single character and looking at the action and the other characters from his/her point of view. This is the way an actor prepares for performance, creating a personality who can have only a partial notion of what is going on, and it asks for a student's inventive imagination and creative writing.

The two methods—both useful in different ways—are really complementary to each other, and for both of them it can be very helpful to re-frame the character's speeches *in your own words*, using the vocabulary and idiom of everyday parlance.

Suggestions

a) from 'outside' the character

B1 'The first scene tells all.' Describe your first impressions of any one or two of these characters, and explain how (if at all) your opinion changes during the course of the play:

Don Pedro	Leonato
Beatrice	Benedick
Claudio	Hero

B2   Compare and contrast the characters of

a) Beatrice and Hero
b) Benedick and Claudio
c) Don Pedro and Leonato
d) Dogberry and Verges

B3   Distinguish between the characters and functions of

a) Margaret and Ursula
b) Borachio and Conrad

B3   'Leonato shows more concern for his status than for his daughter.' Do you agree?

B4   Do you agree that 'Benedick has constructed a character for himself ('I will live a bachelor', *1*, 1, 224), and the real man cannot show through until he declares his love for Beatrice'?

B5   'She cannot endure to hear tell of a husband' (*2*, 1, 322). Is Beatrice afraid of men or of marriage?

B6   'Hath Leonato any son, my lord?' (*1*, 1, 268). What sort of lover is Claudio?

B7   'I am a plain-dealing villain' (*1*, 3, 27–8): is this enough to account for the character of Don John?

B8   'The role is too big for the man—but the character of Dogberry is greater than any ordinary policeman.' Do you agree?

b) from 'inside' the character.

B9 Welcome to Messina! As any one of these characters writing the day's entry in your diary, describe your thoughts and feelings when Don Pedro and his company arrived at Leonato's house. Remember that you have all met before, and speculate about what might happen during the prince's visit:

Claudio	Hero
Benedick	Beatrice
Don John	Leonato

B10 Even though there is no more than 'a just sevennight' between the betrothal and their marriage, Claudio and Hero can find plenty of time to write poems and letters to each other. Compose some of these.

B11 'Good Lord, for alliance!' In the character of Beatrice (writing in your diary, or in a letter to a friend) explain your reaction when Claudio addressed you as 'cousin' (2, 1, 295).

B12 Why is Don Pedro so quick (1, 1, 292) to respond to Claudio's request: ' 'Tis once. Thou lovest'. In his diary, or in a letter (perhaps to Claudio's uncle in Messina), give an account of Don Pedro's feelings for Claudio.

B13 From outside these love affairs, Don John has an acute perception of events and characters, and writes satiric verses to ridicule them. Compose some of these.

B15 The masked ball, the refusal in the church, and 'resurrection' of Hero—all these are *shared* events, but every character's reaction to them is his/her own and confided in personal diaries or letters to absent friends. Choose any one of the play's characters (including the silent servants) and describe the settings and the actions from her/his point of view.

B16 Friar Francis defends his course of action in a letter to his ecclesiastical superiors.

B17 The sexton writes a report on Dogberry's handling of 'The Case of the Deformed Thief'.

B18 Benedick and Beatrice are convicted by their own hands:

> **Claudio**
> . . . here's a paper written in his hand,
> A halting sonnet of his own pure brain,
> Fashioned to Beatrice.

Hero
And here's another,
Writ in my cousin's hand, stol'n from her pocket,
Containing her affection unto Benedick.   (5, 4, 86–90)

Produce the evidence.

B19 'A View from Below Stairs': Margaret tells how she was deceived by Borachio.

B20 Don Pedro muses on Benedick's last words to him—'Prince, thou art sad. Get thee a wife, get thee a wife' (5, 4, 121–2).

C   Activities

These can involve two or more students, preferably working *away from* the desk or study-table. They can help students to develop a sense of drama and the dramatic aspects of Shakespeare's play—which was written to be *performed*, not read!

C1   Act the play—or at least part of it! Read aloud the 'deception' scenes where first Benedick, then Beatrice, is persuaded that the other is desperately in love with him/her. Discard your texts, and act out the scenes in your own words.

C2   'By my troth, niece, thou wilt never get thee a husband if thou be so shrewd of thy tongue' (2, 1, 16–17). Devise a scene in which Leonato and Antonio discuss Beatrice's attitude to marriage, the responsibilities of parents and guardians, and the behaviour of the younger generation.

C3   Don Pedro promises Claudio that he will act as go-between in the courtship of Hero:

I will assume thy part in some disguise,
And tell fair Hero I am Claudio.
And in her bosom I'll unclasp my heart . . .
Then after to her father will I break,
And the conclusion is, she shall be thine.   (1, 1, 295–301)

Supplying your own lines (either in blank verse or in modern prose), act out these conversations.

C4   Borachio promises that Claudio and Don Pedro shall 'see me at [Hero's] chamber window, hear me call Margaret Hero, hear Margaret term me Claudio' (2, 2, 39–41). Improvise this scene.

C5 'The Wedding of the Year.' Imagine that the wedding of Hero and Claudio is taking place in the twentieth century, and give it the treatment it would receive today—full media coverage, with much speculation about 'the dress' (whose design must be kept secret until the wedding day); spotlight on the early days and family relationships of bride and groom, marriage guidance counselling from Friar Francis. The reporters are all in position when Claudio drops his bombshell. Stop Press! Devise headlines and quick dramatic paragraph/news flashes for early editions, followed up later by interviews with anybody who might have been present in the church at the time, or outside Leonato's house the night before the wedding.

C6 There must have been some kind of confrontation in which Don Pedro and Claudio were convinced of Hero's guilt by Borachio's villainy, 'which did confirm any slander that Don John had made' (*Act 3*, Scene 3). Invent such an episode.

C7 'Don John on Trial', 'Prince's brother accused of slander', 'Why did he do it?' When the excitement of the double wedding is over, the characters have time to ask questions. Present the trial of Don John (perhaps with modern media coverage).

D   Context Questions

In written examinations, these questions present you with short passages from the play and ask you to explain them. They are intended to test your knowledge of the play and your understanding of its words. Usually you have to make a choice of passages: there may be five on the paper, and you are asked to choose three. Be very sure that you know exactly how many passages you must choose. Study the ones offered to you, and select those you feel most certain of. Make your answers accurate and concise—don't waste time writing more than the examiner is asking for.

D1   Tush, tush, man, never fleer and jest at me.
I speak not like a dotard nor a fool,
As under privilege of age to brag
What I have done being young, or what would do
Were I not old.

(i) Who is speaking, and who is addressed? Who else is present?
(ii) What has happened to distress the speaker?

(iii) What is the old man offering to do?

(iv) What happens next?

D2   One word, sir. Our watch, sir, have indeed comprehended two auspicious persons, and we would have them this morning examined before your worship.

(i) Who is the speaker, and to whom is he speaking?

(ii) What is 'the watch'?

(iii) Who are the 'two auspicious persons'?

(iv) What does the speaker mean by 'auspicious'?

D3   You have of late stood out against your brother, and he hath ta'en you newly into his grace, where it is impossible you should take true root but by the fair weather that you make yourself.

(i) Who is the speaker, and to whom is he speaking?

(ii) Who is referred to as 'your brother'?

(iii) What has happened recently between the brothers?

(iv) Where do these characters go next?

D4   O god of love! I know he doth deserve

As much as may be yielded to a man,

But nature never fram'd a woman's heart

Of prouder stuff than that of ——.

Disdain and scorn ride sparkling in her eyes,

Misprising what they look on, and her wit

Values itself so highly that to her

All matter else seems weak. She cannot love,

Nor take no shape nor project of affection,

She is so self-endear'd.

(i) Who is speaking, and which characters are listening?

(ii) Who is referred to as 'he', and who is '——'?

(iii) What will be the immediate effect of these words?

(iv) Who is the 'god of love'?

E   Comprehension and Appreciation Questions

These also present passages from the play and ask questions about them; again you often have a choice of passages, but the extracts are much longer than those presented as context questions. A detailed knowledge of the language of the play is required here, and you must be able to express unusual or archaic phrases in your own words; you may also be expected to comment critically on the dramatic techniques of the passage and the poetic effectiveness of Shakespeare's language.

E1   **Claudio**
                      . . . Father, by your leave,
Will you with free and unconstrained soul
Give me this maid, your daughter?
          Leonato
As freely, son, as God did give her me.
          Claudio
And what have I to give you back whose worth   5
May counterpoise this rich and precious gift?
          Don Pedro
Nothing, unless you render her again.
          Claudio
Sweet Prince, you learn me noble thankfulness.
There, Leonato, take her back again.
Give not this rotten orange to your friend!   10
She's but the sign and semblance of her honour.
Behold how like a maid she blushes here.
O, what authority and show of truth
Can cunning sin cover itself withal!
Comes not that blood as modest evidence   15
To witness simple virtue? Would you not swear—
All you that see her—that she were a maid,
By these exterior shows? But she is none.
She knows the heat of a luxurious bed.
Her blush is guiltiness, not modesty.   20
          Leonato
What do you mean, my lord?
          Claudio
                              Not to be married,
Nor to knit my soul to an approved wanton.
          Leonato
Dear my lord, if you in your own proof
Have vanquish'd the resistance of her youth
And made defeat of her virginity—   25
          Claudio
I know what you would say. If I have known her,
You will say she did embrace me as a husband,
And so extenuate the forehand sin.
No, Leonato,
I never tempted her with word too large,   30
But as a brother to his sister show'd
Bashful sincerity and comely love.

Hero

And seem'd I ever otherwise to you?

Claudio

Out on thy seeming! I will write against it.

(i) What is the meaning of '*counterpoise*' (line 6); '*luxurious*' (line 19); '*approved*' (line 22); '*wanton*' (line 22); '*large*' (line 30)?

(ii) In your own words, express the meaning of lines 13–14 ('O, what authority . . . withal') and line 28 ('so extenuate . . . sin').

(iii) Comment on the dramatic qualities of this passage.

(iv) Discuss the importance of 'seeming' in *Much Ado About Nothing*.

E2   **Benedick**

Lady Beatrice, have you wept all this while?

Beatrice

Yea, and I will weep a while longer.

Benedick

I will not desire that.

Beatrice

You have no reason; I do it freely.

Benedick

Surely I do believe your fair cousin is wronged.   5

Beatrice

Ah, how much might the man deserve of me that would right her!

Benedick

Is there any way to show such friendship?

Beatrice

A very even way, but no such friend.

Benedick

May a man do it?   10

Beatrice

It is a man's office, but not yours.

Benedick

I do love nothing in the world so well as you. Is not that strange?

Beatrice

As strange as the thing I know not. It were as possible for me to say I loved nothing so well as you. But believe me   15 not, and yet I lie not. I confess nothing nor I deny nothing; I am sorry for my cousin.

Benedick

By my sword, Beatrice, thou lovest me.

Beatrice

Do not swear and eat it.

Benedick

I will swear by it that you love me, and I will make him   20
eat it that says I love not you.

Beatrice

Will you not eat your word?

Benedick

With no sauce that can be devised to it. I protest I love
thee.

Beatrice

Why then, God forgive me.

Benedick

What offence, sweet Beatrice?   25

Beatrice

You have stayed me in a happy hour. I was about to
protest I loved you.

Benedick

And do it with all thy heart.

Beatrice

I love you with so much of my heart that none is left to
protest.   30

Benedick

Come, bid me do anything for thee.

Beatrice

Kill Claudio.

Benedick

Ha! Not for the wide world.

Beatrice

You kill me to deny it. Farewell.

Benedick

[*Barring her way*] Tarry, sweet Beatrice.   35

(i) What is the meaning of '*even*' (line 9); '*office*' (line 11);
    '*protest*' (line 23); '*happy*' (line 26)?

(ii) What qualities of the two characters are shown in this
     passage?

(iii) Comment on the different dramatic tensions in this
      passage.

F   Essays

These will usually give you a specific topic to discuss, or perhaps a question that must be answered, in writing, *with a reasoned argument*. They *never* want you to tell the story of the play—so don't! Your examiner—or teacher—has read the play, and does not need to be reminded of it. Relevant quotations will always help you to make your points more strongly.

F1   'Friendship is constant in all other things Save in the office and affairs of love' (2, 1, 163–4). How important is male friendship as a theme in the play?

F2   What do you learn from *Much Ado About Nothing* of the qualities and conduct of a romantic lover?

F3   The wedding of Claudio and Hero cannot be until 'Monday . . . which is hence a just sevennight' (2, 1, 331–2). Work out the time sequences in the play.

F4   'Listening in to private conversations is responsible for all the trouble in Messina.' How true is this?

F5   'Yet sinn'd I not But in mistaking' (5, 1, 267–8). Can Claudio excuse himself so easily?

F6   'Dogberry's incompetence is just enough! If he had been more efficient, there would have been no play.' Do you agree?

F7   'The comedy of Beatrice and Benedick is more important than the tragedy of Claudio and Hero—yet this should be the play's main concern.' Is this your opinion?

F8   Comment on the use of masks in *Much Ado About Nothing*.

G   Projects

In some schools, students are required to do more 'free-ranging' work, which takes them outside the text—but which should always be relevant to the play. Such Projects may demand skills other than reading and writing: design and artwork, for instance, may be involved. Sometimes a 'portfolio' of work is assembled over a considerable period of time; and this can be offered to the examiner for assessment.

The availability of resources will, obviously, do much to determine the nature of the Projects; but this is something that only the local teachers will understand. However, there is always help to be found in libraries, museums, and art galleries.

Suggested Subjects

G1   Elizabethan masks.
G2   Elizabethan wedding dresses.
G3   Policing the city in Shakespeare's day.
G4   'the fashion of a new doublet' (2, 3, 17): male costumes in Shakespeare's day.
G5   Beatrice and Benedick: great performances of the past.
G6   Elizabethan dancing.

Background

England c. 1599

When Shakespeare was writing *Much Ado About Nothing*, many people still believed that the sun went round the earth. They were taught that this was a divinely ordered scheme of things, and that—in England—God had instituted a Church and ordained a Monarchy for the right government of the land and the populace.

'The past is a foreign country; they do things differently there.'

L. P. Hartley

Government

For most of Shakespeare's life, the reigning monarch of England was Queen Elizabeth I. With her counsellors and ministers, she governed the nation (population less than six million) from London, although fewer than half a million people inhabited the capital city. In the rest of the country, law and order were maintained by the land-owners and enforced by their deputies. The average man had no vote, and his wife had no rights at all.

Religion

At this time, England was a Christian country. All children were baptized, soon after they were born, into the Church of England; they were taught the essentials of the Christian faith, and instructed in their duty to God and to humankind. Marriages were performed, and funerals conducted, only by the licensed clergy and in accordance with the Church's rites and ceremonies. Attendance at divine service was compulsory; absences (without good—medical—reason) could be punished by fines. By such means, the authorities were able to keep some check on the populace—recording births, marriages, and deaths; being alert to any religious nonconformity, which could be politically dangerous; and ensuring a minimum of orthodox instruction through the official 'Homilies' which were regularly preached from the pulpits of all parish churches throughout the realm.

Following Henry VIII's break away from the Church of Rome, all people in England were able to hear the church services *in their own language*. The Book of Common Prayer was used in every church, and an English translation of the Bible was read aloud in public. The Christian religion had never been so well taught before!

Education

School education reinforced the Church's teaching. From the age of four, boys might attend the 'petty school' (French '*petite école*') to learn the rudiments of reading and writing along with a few prayers; some schools also included work with numbers. At the age of seven, the boy was ready for the grammar school (if his father was willing and able to pay the fees).

Here a thorough grounding in Latin grammar was followed by translation work and the study of Roman authors, paying attention as much to style as to matter. The arts of fine writing were thus inculcated from early youth. A very few students proceeded to university; these were either clever scholarship boys, or else the sons of noblemen. Girls stayed at home, and acquired domestic and social skills—cooking, sewing, perhaps even music. The lucky ones might learn to read and write.

Language

At the start of the sixteenth century the English had a very poor opinion of their own language: there was little serious writing in English, and hardly any literature. Latin was the language of international scholarship, and Englishmen admired the eloquence of the Romans. They made many translations, and in this way they extended the resources of their own language, increasing its vocabulary and stretching its grammatical structures. French, Italian, and Spanish works were also translated and, for the first time, there were English versions of the Bible. By the end of the century, English was a language to be proud of: it was rich in synonyms, capable of infinite variety and subtlety, and ready for all kinds of word-play—especially the *puns*, for which Elizabethan English is renowned.

Drama

The great art-form of the Elizabethan and Jacobean age was its drama. The Elizabethans inherited a tradition of play-acting from the Middle Ages, and they reinforced this by reading and translating the Roman playwrights. At the beginning of the sixteenth century plays were performed by groups of actors, all-male companies (boys acted the female roles) who travelled from town to town, setting up their stages in open places (such as inn-yards) or, with the permission of the owner, in the hall of some noble house. The touring companies continued in the provinces into the seventeenth century; but in London, in 1576, a new building was erected for the performance of plays. This was the Theatre, the first purpose-built playhouse in England. Other playhouses followed, (including the Globe, where most of Shakespeare's plays were performed), and the English drama reached new heights of eloquence.

There were those who disapproved, of course. The theatres, which brought large crowds together, could encourage the spread of disease—and dangerous ideas. During the summer, when the plague was at its worst, the playhouses were closed. A constant censorship was imposed, more or less severe at different times. The Puritan faction tried to close down the theatres, but—partly because there was royal favour for the drama, and partly because the buildings were outside the city limits—they did not succeed until 1642.

Theatre

From contemporary comments and sketches—most particularly a drawing by a Dutch visitor, Johannes de Witt—it is possible to form some idea of the typical Elizabethan playhouse for which most of Shakespeare's plays were written. Hexagonal in shape, it had three roofed galleries encircling an open courtyard. The plain, high stage projected into the yard, where it was surrounded by the audience of standing 'groundlings'. At the back were two doors for the actors' entrances and exits; and above these doors was a balcony—useful for a musicians' gallery or for the acting of scenes 'above'. Over the stage was a thatched roof, supported on two pillars, forming a canopy—which seems to have been painted with the sun, moon, and stars for the 'heavens'.

Underneath was space (concealed by curtaining) which could be used by characters ascending and descending through a trapdoor in the stage. Costumes and properties were kept backstage in the 'tiring house'. The actors dressed lavishly, often wearing the secondhand clothes bestowed by rich patrons. Stage properties were important for defining a location, but the dramatist's own words were needed to explain the time of day, since all performances took place in the early afternoon.

A replica of Shakespeare's own theatre, the Globe, has been built in London, and stands in Southwark, almost exactly on the Bankside site of the original.

Further Reading

Editions:

Excellent introductions to *Much Ado About Nothing* are to be found in:

Foakes, R. A. (ed.), *Much Ado About Nothing* (New Penguin Shakespeare, Harmondsworth, 1968).
Humphreys, A. R. (ed.), *Much Ado About Nothing* (Arden Shakespeare, London, 1981).

Critical Works:

Brown, J. Russell (ed.), *'Much Ado About Nothing' and 'As You Like It': A Casebook* (Macmillan, 1979).
Davis, Walter R. (ed.), *Twentieth Century Interpretations of 'Much Ado About Nothing'*, (London, 1969).
Lerner, Laurence (ed.), *Shakespeare's Comedies: An Anthology of Modern Criticism*, (London, 1967).
Muir, K. (ed.), *Shakespeare: The Comedies; A collection of Critical Essays*, (London, 1965).
Dusinberre, Juliet, *Shakespeare and the Nature of Women* (London, 1975).
Leggatt, Alexander, *Shakespeare's Comedy of Love* (London, 1974).
Mulryne, J. R., *Shakespeare: 'Much Ado About Nothing'* (Arnold's Studies in English Literature, 16; London, 1965).
Palmer, John, *Comic Characters in Shakespeare* (London, 1946).

Sources:

Bullough, Geoffrey (ed.), *Narrative and Dramatic Sources of Shakespeare*, vol. ii (London, 1958).
Muir, Kenneth, *The Sources of Shakespeare's Plays* (London, 1977).

Additional background reading:

Bate, Jonathan, *The Genius of Shakespeare* (Picador [Macmillan], 1997).

Blake, N. F., *Shakespeare's Language: an Introduction*, (London, 1983).

Muir, K., and Schoenbaum, S., *A New Companion to Shakespeare Studies*, (Cambridge, 1971).

Schoenbaum, S., *William Shakespeare: A Documentary Life*, (Oxford, 1975).

Thomson, Peter, *Shakespeare's Theatre*, (London, 1983).

William Shakespeare, 1564–1616

Elizabeth I was Queen of England when Shakespeare was born in 1564. He was the son of a tradesman who made and sold gloves in the small town of Stratford-upon-Avon, and he was educated at the grammar school in that town. Shakespeare did not go to university when he left school, but worked, perhaps, in his father's business. When he was eighteen he married Anne Hathaway, who became the mother of his daughter, Susanna, in 1583, and of twins in 1585.

There is nothing exciting, or even unusual, in this story; and from 1585 until 1592 there are no documents that can tell us anything at all about Shakespeare. But we have learned that in 1592 he was known in London, and that he had become both an actor and a playwright.

We do not know when Shakespeare wrote his first play, and indeed we are not sure of the order in which he wrote his works. If you look on page 127 at the list of his writings and their approximate dates, you will see how he started by writing plays on subjects taken from the history of England. No doubt this was partly because he was always an intensely patriotic man—but he was also a very shrewd business-man. He could see that the theatre audiences enjoyed being shown their own history, and it was certain that he would make a profit from this kind of drama.

The plays in the next group are mainly comedies, with romantic love-stories of young people who fall in love with one another, and at the end of the play marry and live happily ever after.

At the end of the sixteenth century the happiness disappears, and Shakespeare's plays become melancholy, bitter, and tragic. This change may have been caused by some sadness in the writer's life (one of his twins died in 1596). Shakespeare, however, was not the only writer whose works at this time were very serious. The whole of England was facing a crisis. Queen Elizabeth I was growing old. She was greatly loved, and the people were sad to think she must soon die; they were also afraid, for the queen had never married, and so there was no child to succeed her.

When James I came to the throne in 1603, Shakespeare continued to write serious drama—the great tragedies and the plays based on Roman history for which he is most famous. Finally, before he retired from the theatre, he wrote another set of comedies. These all have the same theme: they tell of happiness which is lost, and then found again.

Shakespeare returned from London to Stratford, his home town. He was rich and successful, and he owned one of the biggest houses in the town. He died in 1616.

Shakespeare also wrote two long poems, and a collection of sonnets. The sonnets describe two love-affairs, but we do not know who the lovers were. Although there are many public documents concerned with his career as a writer and a business-man, Shakespeare has hidden his personal life from us. A nineteenth-century poet, Matthew Arnold, addressed Shakespeare in a poem, and wrote 'We ask and ask—Thou smilest, and art still'.

There is not even a trustworthy portrait of the world's greatest dramatist.

Approximate order of composition of Shakespeare's works

Period	Comedies	History plays	Tragedies	Poems
I	Comedy of Errors	Henry VI, part 1	Titus Andronicus	
1594	Taming of the Shrew	Henry VI, part 2		
	Two Gentlemen of Verona	Henry VI, part 3		
		Richard III		Venus and Adonis
	Love's Labour's Lost	King John		Rape of Lucrece
II	Midsummer Night's Dream	Richard II	Romeo and Juliet	Sonnets
1599	Merchant of Venice	Henry IV, part 1		
	Merry Wives of Windsor	Henry IV, part 2		
	Much Ado About Nothing			
	As You Like It	Henry V		
III	Twelfth Night		Julius Caesar	
1608	Troilus and Cressida		Hamlet	
	Measure for Measure		Othello	
	All's Well That Ends Well		Timon of Athens	
			King Lear	
			Macbeth	
			Antony and Cleopatra	
			Coriolanus	
IV	Pericles			
1613	Cymbeline			
	The Winter's Tale	Henry VIII		
	The Tempest			